SPECIAL REPORT

AF833606

The New Stage of Perestroika

Abel Aganbegyan
Timor Timofeyev

Routledge
Taylor & Francis Group
LONDON AND NEW YORK

First published 1988 by Westview Press

Published 2019 by Routledge
52 Vanderbilt Avenue, New York, NY 10017
2 Park Square, Milton Park, Abingdon, Oxon OX14 4RN

Routledge is an imprint of the Taylor & Francis Group, an informa business

ISBN 13: 978-0-367-29441-0 (hbk)
ISBN 13: 978-0-367-30987-9 (pbk)

Table of Contents

Foreword 5
Whitney MacMillan

I. **Introduction: Perestroika and Economic Security** 9
John Edwin Mroz

II. **Acceleration and Perestroika** 25
Abel Aganbegyan

III. **The Social Aspects of Perestroika** 45
Timor Timofeyev

IV. **Appendix: "Principles of Restructuring: Revolutionary Nature of Thinking and Acting"** 61
Pravda, April 5, 1988

About the Authors 77

Foreword

The Institute for East-West Security Studies (IEWSS) is pleased to present this publication on *The New Stage of Perestroika*, featuring two papers by prominent Soviets—Academician Abel Aganbegyan, Head of the Economics Branch of the USSR Academy of Sciences and General Secretary Mikhail Gorbachev's chief economic advisor, and Professor Timor Timofeyev, Director of the Institute of International Labor Studies. The thoughtful introduction by my colleague, John Edwin Mroz, President of the Institute for East-West Security Studies, explains why the IEWSS publications agenda encompasses the subject of the reforms being undertaken in the USSR.

A series of discussions have taken place this winter and spring between staff members and research fellows of the IEWSS and a group of experts from the USSR, including the authors of this volume, on the subject of *perestroika*, Soviet New Thinking and the linkage between domestic and international economic problems and policies. These discussions and this publication are the first step in the development of an ongoing process of cooperation between the IEWSS and several security specialists in the USSR. The seriousness with which we regard the cooperation between the Institute and our colleagues in the USSR is reflected in the joint decision to produce such a publication on relatively short notice.

The volume provides useful insights on the relationship between domestic economic reform in the Soviet Union and the social aspects of the reform process. This relationship has not received sufficient attention in the West and it is hoped that the papers in this report will serve to further the agenda for discussion between the East and the West.

The papers in this volume are a fitting public response by the

Soviet Union to the Institute's year-long project on Soviet New Thinking. The shift in long-standing Soviet positions on a range of key issues challenged the West to respond and necessitated an examination of Western policy towards the USSR and the assumptions behind them. This led to the formation in January 1987 of the Institute's bipartisan Task Force on Soviet New Thinking, which brought together academics, government officials, businessmen, journalists and lawyers to share their experience in a unique forum. The results of the Task Force's deliberations were published in a widely discussed Report, *How Should America Respond to Gorbachev's Challenge?* This Task Force Report was the first concerted effort in the United States to analyze and evaluate the significance of Mikhail Gorbachev's domestic and foreign policies and their implications for East-West relations, and to produce a series of policy recommendations for the U.S. response to changes in the USSR.

The Report was released at a major international conference in St. Paul, Minnesota, convened at Macalester College, October 9–11, 1987, on "The Implications of Soviet New Thinking." A number of important statements and observations were made at the conference by such persons as Foreign Minister and Vice Chancellor of the Federal Republic of Germany Hans-Dietrich Genscher, U.S Deputy Secretary of State John Whitehead, Deputy Foreign Minister of the German Democratic Republic Harry Ott, U.S. Senator Bill Bradley, NATO Foreign Ministers Steingrimur Hermannsson of Iceland and Thorvald Stoltenberg of Norway, Pepsico Chairman of the Executive Committee Donald Kendall, and Jim Giffen, President of the U.S.-USSR Trade & Economic Council. The publication resulting from that conference, *The Implications of Soviet New Thinking,* has received a very positive response among the media and the policy communities in East and West.

This volume, the third in the Institute's series on Soviet New Thinking, is an appropriate Soviet response to the first two publications, appearing at a critical juncture in U.S.-Soviet relations, as President Reagan and General Secretary Mikhail Gorbachev prepare to meet in Moscow for their fourth summit. It marks the completion of the Task Force process and it reaffirms the need to continue the reexamination of traditional policy positions in East and West, with the aim of a more constructive relationship.

This publication also heralds the beginning of a multi-year process in which the Institute for East-West Security Studies will engage Americans, Europeans and Soviets in a systematic discussion of the changing relationship between East and West. The Institute views this as an intrinsic part of the institutionalization of dialogue between East and West on ways to create a more stable and cooperative relationship.

Thus, in October 1988 the Institute will launch an East-West Task Force on "Seeking Security in the 1990s," composed of specialists from the leading capitalist and socialist countries. This Task Force is designed as a policy-oriented vehicle to undertake analysis of the changes in the international system which challenge long-held assumptions about how both sides define and achieve security. We intend the Task Force to generate options for dealing with these changes. The purpose of the Task Force will be to raise the level of dialogue between East and West to a more fundamental discussion about the future of the relationship of the capitalist and socialist systems and their responses to global problems of serious concern to both. The Task Force is intended to demonstrate a new level of cooperation between East and West and provide intellectual leadership on the security agenda in the 1990s. This publication provides an interesting beginning to the discussion on stability and change in the domestic environment and inevitably raises questions about the link between domestic and international policies.

I am grateful to my colleagues at the Institute, in particular our President, John Edwin Mroz, and his staff, especially F. Stephen Larrabee, Claire Gordon, Peter B. Kaufman and Keith Wind, who are responsible for the rapid and timely release of this publication. The Institute wishes to thank the Miriam and Ira D. Wallach Foundation and the Stephen C. Swid and Nan G. Swid Foundation for generously supporting the publication and dissemination of this volume, and the John D. and Catherine T. MacArthur Foundation for its support of the Institute's Publications Program. Special thanks are also paid to Dr. Georgio Dazzi, head of the Moscow office of FATA European Group, for his hospitality and communications assistance. We are pleased to sponsor publication of these papers as a further contribution to the East-West debate. The broader and deeper the debate in both East and West about the future of our relationship, the more likely we are to reach some important decisions that will benefit all.

Whitney MacMillan
Chairman of the Board, Cargill, Inc.
Co-Chairman of the Board of Directors,
Institute for East-West Security Studies
May 1988

Introduction: Perestroika and Economic Security

by
John Edwin Mroz

This publication, *The New Stage of Perestroika*, marks the beginning of a new phase in the substantive work of the Institute for East-West Security Studies, involving close cooperation between the staff and fellows at the IEWSS and our colleagues in the Soviet Union. The papers written for this volume by Academician Abel Aganbegyan, Head of the Economics Branch of the USSR Academy of Sciences and one of General Secretary Mikhail Gorbachev's chief economic advisors, and Professor Timor Timofeyev, Director of the Institute for International Labor Studies, emanated from a series of discussions in Moscow and New York in the winter and spring of 1988. The central focus of these discussions was the intrinsic linkage between Soviet radical domestic reforms—*perestroika*—and international economic changes, and their relationship to both internal stability and international security.

Since General Secretary Gorbachev came to power in March 1985, a significant shift in Soviet attitudes towards domestic and foreign affairs has taken place. The surprisingly candid acknowledgment of domestic difficulties and the recognition that social and economic conditions must not be allowed to deteriorate further has had a profound effect on the direction of Soviet domestic and foreign policy. The Soviet leadership seems to have recognized that the strength of a nation can no longer rest solely on powerful defenses and heavy investment in the military sector, particularly when the domestic economic situation is unsatisfactory and the possibility of losing further ground within the global economy is increasing. Discerning the growing importance of economic performance as the key to the strength and stability of the country, the Soviet leadership appears to be firmly committed to subordinating its foreign policy to the imperative of domestic reform and economic modernization. In both domestic and foreign policy, the Soviet Union is in a transitional stage, testing new approaches and creating new structures.

The Soviet leadership and academic community seem to be searching for ways to realign domestic economic and social relations. The papers in this volume present an assessment of the development and accomplishments of *perestroika* in its first three years. Western readers will find particularly interesting the discussion of the social aspects of the reform process. This is an area which in the past has not received adequate attention in the West. This introduction examines the delicate relationship between change and stability in the Soviet economy, taking into account the role of social factors in the overall domestic reform process and the broader question of the Soviet Union's role in the international community.

Rethinking in the Domestic Field

The link between domestic economic and social conditions and internal stability poses a challenge for the Soviet leadership. This pivotal relationship has directly influenced the way Moscow has sought to restructure the Soviet economy and to proceed with the current reform process in the Soviet Union. Western observers have long argued that severe economic and technological inadequacies as well as declining living standards could undermine the stability of the Soviet Union. The USSR cannot continue indefinitely on the path of "technological dualism," characterized by low-quality civilian technology and high-technology production in the military sector. Reversing these trends will require major structural reform and the introduction of new concepts in foreign policy.

Both Academician Aganbegyan and Professor Timofeyev acknowledge the failure of previous leaderships to respond to changes in the economic situation. As Professor Timofeyev notes, "For several decades Soviet theorists proceeded from the belief that everything about socialism, especially its economic mechanism, had emerged, and required no alteration, from the ideas of the 1920s and 1930s." The willingness of the present Soviet leadership to confront this situation and its commitment to reform has surprised the majority of Western specialists.

Innovative concepts have entered the Soviet language of domestic reform and have come to assume major importance in the reform process. The all-encompassing notion of *perestroika,* involving restructuring of the economic, social, cultural and political mechanisms of the country, characterizes the whole reform process. The term *uskorenie,* or acceleration, which is less well known in the West, expresses the need to raise the level of—and assimilate—scientific-technological methods in production together with the urgency of improving social conditions. Western observers are struck by the apparent contradiction between the two concepts—*perestroika* and *uskorenie.* By definition, any form of restructuring causes disruption and dislocation. Real *uskorenie,* implying rapid growth, is more likely to be the result of reform, rather than its cause. In the short run, it is hard to see how acceleration will engender *perestroika* and conversely, how *perestroika* will engender acceleration. A fuller discussion of this relationship between Soviet specialists and their Western counterparts would be useful.

Soviet and Western economists have challenged the deeply entrenched Soviet growth strategy. Soviet economist Vasilii Selyunin advocates slower economic growth in the short run in favor of developing the consumer-goods sector.[1] He argues that in the Soviet context economic acceleration is not likely to generate improvements in living standards and it is with the latter that the Soviet leadership should be concerned. If restructuring is to succeed it must enjoy the support of the people. Therefore the economy must be changed so that the consumer-goods sector represents a larger share of total output. A wider variety of higher quality goods from which to choose provides incentives for an increase in labor productivity for all sectors of the economy. Academician Aganbegyan, in his paper, questions the obsessive concern with consumerism and outlines measures which have been taken, for example, in the health and housing sectors to improve conditions for workers. Professor Timofeyev, in his paper, points to the need for

1. Vasilii Selyunin, "Tempy rosta na vesakh potrebleniya," *Sotsialisticheskaya industriya,* January 5, 1988, pp. 2–3.

addressing further resource allocation and investment strategy and their relationship to improving living conditions of the workers.

Any society faces certain risks in the introduction of radical policies. The Soviet population has experienced fluctuating periods of reform and retrenchment; many Soviet citizens are wary of making sacrifices and fear that taking initiative and greater responsibility may threaten their positions. The rhetorical emphasis on acceleration is perhaps a form of reassurance for the population, which thinks in terms of improvements in living standards. Some in the West say that current government policies can be interpreted as breaking the long-standing "social contract"—the tacit understanding between state and society whereby society exchanges compliance with the system and acceptance of low living standards in exchange for minimum levels of social security (basic food, housing, employment, health care and pension). Should this be true, the consequences of forging a new social contract could involve both a protracted and socially disruptive process.

Gorbachev acknowledges that in order for the Soviet Union to retain its position as a global power, structural reform of the system is an absolute necessity. The Gorbachev leadership effectively communicates the stark and unpleasant realities of the domestic situation in order to convince the population that there is no alternative to restructuring. The leadership openly speaks of the poor economic performance, declining growth rates, low productivity and poor quality of goods as well as the appalling conditions in the health-care and housing sectors, underlining in particular the deterioration which has occurred since the early 1960s.[2]

In his February 18, 1988, speech to the Central Committee plenum, General Secretary Gorbachev pointed out that "If we look at the economic indicators of growth omitting these factors [the price increase of oil sold abroad and alcohol sales at home], we will see that practically over four five-year plan periods there was no increase in the absolute increment of the national income and it even began declining in the early

2. See Abel Aganbegyan, "Slagaemie Perestroiki," *Nauka i Zhizn'* 3 (March 1988), pp. 2–15.

1980s."[3] It would appear that the motivation behind the disclosure of such information is precisely the need to show the gravity of the economic situation. If structural reform is to succeed, there must be widespread consensus on the nature of the crisis facing the system.

The leadership has tried to enlist the active support and participation of the Soviet people in the campaign for reform, showing that there is no alternative to the breadth of Gorbachev's vision. Many were surprised that the media has assumed a new, important role in this process with the *glasnost'* campaign. Highly critical letters-to-the-editor and surprisingly frank reporting of domestic news, social and economic conditions, as well as foreign news have led to a lively exchange of ideas. The Soviet press has assisted in raising the awareness of the populace about the imperative to restructure while at the same time making it more difficult to publicly resist the reform program. The encouragement of public participation in *perestroika* and *glasnost'* has led to a surge of public interest in environmental and social issues. Gorbachev needs to create an atmosphere of what the Soviets now call "dynamic stability," preparing the population for the introduction of reform measures and allowing it the flexibility to participate in the changing environment.

The Human Factor

Professor Timofeyev and Academician Aganbegyan present an important new dimension to the Western reader with their central focus on the "human factor" and the social aspects of reform. This emphasis echoes the desire of the leadership to stimulate individual interest and care in the "public product," thereby unifying individual and common interests. The importance attached to this issue reflects the search for a balance between the logic and order of the planned economy and the need to acknowledge and accommodate the human response, involving the question of motivation and individual initiative.

3. Mikhail S. Gorbachev, *The Ideology of Renewal for Revolutionary Restructuring*, February 18, 1988 (Moscow: Novosti, 1988), p. 36.

It would appear that striking a "dynamic equilibrium" between these factors would lessen the impact of instability that any such radical reform process intrinsically stimulates.

The discussion of the human factor has led to the increased recognition of "interests" in society and the need for diversity of opinions on public issues. According to Academician Tatyana Zaslavskaya, the influential economic sociologist, "The existing system of management of the human factor is distinguished for its extreme rigidity, lack of flexibility and poor adaptability to changing conditions of place and time."[4] The discussion of such issues has led to a heated and, to an unprecedented degree, open debate among economists, sociologists and the leadership over such questions as wage differentials, price increases and changes in employment. Wage-leveling, heavily subsidized food prices and full employment have for decades been basic tenets of Soviet socialism and have guaranteed the economic security of Soviet citizens.

Western observers have noted that in the past the Soviet leadership sought to achieve political stability by promoting equality at the cost of efficiency and ensuring near-absolute economic security. It appears to Western observers that the Soviet leadership has accepted the fact that this is no longer a viable option. Continuing poor economic performance at the end of the 1970s was seen as possibly leading to serious problems. The Soviet leadership recognized what Gorbachev and others have called the "pre-crisis situation." They decided to launch a modernization program, well aware that this course could engender a period of fierce bureaucratic resistance and important difficulties.

A rather widely held theory has emerged in the Soviet Union that previous reforms failed primarily because of bureaucratic resistance centered in the ministries. This theory seems to echo explanations given for the purges of the party and industrial managers in the late 1920s and 1930s and presents a simplified explanation of a more complex issue. Opposition to change is a major problem. Efforts to implement

---

4. Interview with Tatyana Zaslavskaya, "The Reconstruction Is for Us," *Moscow News* (English) 9, March 1, 1987, p. 13, translated in *Foreign Broadcast Information Service-Soviet Union* [hereafter *FBIS-SU*], March 18, 1987, p. S5.

perestroika are encountering resistance from those who fear loss of power or privilege as well as from those who are frightened to risk any change in the status quo, preferring the security of present conditions, no matter how bad they are. But reducing the failure of reform to a question of "resistance"—bureaucratic or otherwise, direct or indirect—overlooks deeper systemic obstacles to change.

A new element in the reform debate in the Soviet Union is concerned with the forces against reform and the need to neutralize opposition, while seeking support from those who will benefit from the reform. Significant changes in the existing system of economic relations will lead to changes for different strata of society. According to Academician Zaslavskaya, a reform is not simply worked out and implemented by professionals, but is rather "a complex process of mutual interaction of socioeconomic groups, occupying different positions in social production and following contradictory interests."[5] In the discussions held in New York and Moscow with Soviet colleagues, we only began to address the complex issue of the resistance that the introduction of reform measures is encountering at various levels of society. This is likely to be a problem which could affect both the pace and eventual success of Gorbachev's reform program.

The restructuring of the domestic economy inevitably influences the economic, political and military options of the Soviet leadership in the foreign policy sphere. The relationship of *perestroika* and *uskorenie* on the domestic and international scene as well as its impact on foreign and defense policy deserves further exploration.

Shifts in Soviet Foreign Policy

A process of changes in basic Soviet foreign policy has begun, reflected in both the Soviet theory and language of international relations, as well as in its foreign policy conduct. The changes in long-held Soviet positions—over Afghanistan,

5. Tatyana Zaslavskaya, "Ekonomika skvoz' prizmu sotsiologii," *The Economics and Organization of Industrial Production* (*EKO*) 7 (July 1985), quoted in Ed A. Hewett, *Reforming the Soviet Economy* (Washington, DC: Brookings Institution, 1988), p. 277.

the admission of the existence of asymmetries in conventional forces in Europe, the acceptance of intrusive verification measures and the move towards "reasonable sufficiency" in defense planning—reflect that Soviet foreign policy is influenced both by the changing nature of the international system and the severity of the domestic situation. In many ways, the new thinking in Soviet policy represents a crystallization of tendencies that have long been present in Soviet policy circles. According to Robert Legvold, Director of Columbia University's Harriman Institute, "for more than a decade, members of the Soviet foreign policy establishment . . . have been inventing and shaping ideas like those which Gorbachev now articulates."[6] A move away from the primacy of ideology towards practical considerations seems to be taking place. Soviet Foreign Minister Eduard Shevardnadze notes: "We are people of ideas, but their power should not be higher than considerations of common sense."[7]

The Soviet leadership appears to have concluded that a favorable international environment for the success of economic restructuring is best created on the basis of political accommodation with the United States. New emphasis is being placed on seeking agreement with the West on long-standing security issues. The concept of security is being reinterpreted in a broader way: not only are Soviet officials stressing that a nuclear war cannot under any circumstances be won, they argue that security can no longer be achieved through military means alone. Their newly articulated concept of "reasonable sufficiency" is motivated by economic considerations and a strategic reconsideration of the significance of nuclear weapons. The new approach to security encompasses economic, social, humanitarian and environmental questions as well as military ones.

6. Robert Legvold, "Gorbachev's Foreign Policy: The New Thinking," from "Gorbachev's Foreign Policy: How Should the United States Respond?" *Headline Series* 284 (New York: Foreign Policy Association in cooperation with the Institute for East-West Security Studies, 1988).
7. Speech by Eduard A. Shevardnadze at a meeting of the USSR Ministry of Foreign Affairs Workers Aktiv on July 4, 1987, "An Unconditional Requirement—Turn to Face the Economy," *Vestnik Ministerstva Inostrannykh Del SSSR* 3 (September 10, 1987) in *FBIS-SU*, November 3, 1987, pp. 88–90.

The Soviet concept of "peaceful coexistence" has also been reinterpreted. The recognition of the threat to survival posed by nuclear weapons has led to a subordination of class interests to the priority of global human survival. Peaceful coexistence becomes a condition in which states with different social and political systems have to learn how to live with each other for the indefinite future. Academician Yevgeny Primakov, Director of the Institute of the World Economy and International Relations, argues that interstate relations cannot be the sphere in which the outcome of confrontation between world socialism and world capitalism is settled.[8] Coexistence is now said to imply an order in which relations of confidence and cooperation prevail and global problems can be resolved on a collaborative basis. This appraisal presents both challenges and opportunities for the West.

The Gorbachev leadership increasingly recognizes the multipolar and interdependent character of contemporary international relations. Previously, the "two-world-economy" approach saw two incompatible, rival economies running along parallel tracks with only marginal linkages. Soviet Foreign Minister Shevardnadze has placed the evolving Soviet attitude in a strategic framework. "In reality," he has said, "the division into socialist and capitalist systems of economics, with all the extremely perceptible limitations for us, in no way signifies the absence of mutual penetration. We were drawn into the world economic process long ago, and other of our friends have gone much further. . . . We should be part of the world economic system and we can and are obliged to become so if we accept and assimilate the forms extant in it [the General Agreement on Tariffs and Trade, World Bank membership, etc.]."[9]

This emphasis on interdependence must be placed in a broader framework. The development of communications technology, foreign trade, financial and investment factors and global environmental problems are underlying trends to which all countries, including the Soviet Union, must respond. Isolationist trends have long been prevalent in the Soviet

---

8. Yevgeny Primakov, "Novaya filosofiya vneshnei politiki," *Pravda*, July 9, 1987, p. 4.
9. Shevardnadze, "An Unconditional Requirement—Turn to Face the Economy," in *FBIS-SU*, November 3, 1987, p. 89.

Union with the perception of hostile encirclement. The "two-world-economy" approach was a direct reflection of such attitudes. Although these attitudes are less prominent today, it is likely that the USSR will, for a long time, continue to see (and legitimately so) a challenge to its superpower status and a series of new problems raised by integration into the world economy. However, as economic power becomes an increasingly important determinant of strength, the Soviet Union will find itself under increased pressure to become more fully integrated in the world economy. John Hardt of the Congressional Research Service places the shift in Soviet emphasis towards interdependence in the broader framework of the transition of the Soviet Union to a modern industrial economy. "The Soviet Union and the United States, as large, relatively self-sufficient economies, have not emphasized interdependence and competitiveness in the past."[10]

Gorbachev's commitment to *perestroika* necessitates a durable and predictable framework for the critical resource allocation choices—choices between military investment, civilian investment and civilian consumption—that must be made in the coming decade. This can be brought about through a stable international environment and a decrease in military competition. Since Gorbachev has greater flexibility in foreign policy than in domestic policy, he has sought to translate dramatic results in foreign affairs into political capital and psychological momentum in the domestic sphere. Changing foreign policy postures poses fewer problems than do structural economic reforms. Changing the basic directions of foreign policy has always been a simpler prerogative of the Soviet leadership than changing the economy. There are fewer vested interests involved in foreign policy than in economic affairs, where the power and status of the bureaucracy as well as the economic security of the workers are threatened. It remains to be seen whether Gorbachev can continue to produce successes in the foreign policy arena to compensate for the discomfort caused by the increased responsibility demanded of workers without immediate consumer benefits. The latest statistics indicate that

10. John Hardt, "Perestroika and Interdependence: Toward Modernization and Competitiveness," Comments for the Panel of the U.S.-USSR Trade and Economic Council Meeting, Moscow, April 1988, p. 1.

the short-term growth prospects of the economy are limited and that consumer morale could be further dampened in 1988 as a result of restructuring programs.[11]

There is yet another aspect of this issue. A number of important international factors have contributed to the rethinking of traditional stances in both the East and West. These include the dynamism of the market-economy countries, which has led to a growing gap between capitalist and socialist countries; the intractability of change in the Third World and the growing burden of heavily indebted Third World regimes; and a structural shift in power relations in international politics, with a decrease in superpower influence in an increasingly multipolar world. The growing economic strength of Japan and the Federal Republic of Germany stands in stark contrast to the stagnation in the domestic Soviet economy and the export deficit of the United States. The Soviet technology gap with the West is and has been growing, while at the same time the newly industrialized countries (NICs), such as South Korea, Singapore, Brazil and Taiwan, are assuming an ever more important role in the world economy and rapidly narrowing that same gap between themselves and the Soviet Union. Greater interdependence between East and West, North and South, has refuted the purely 'zero-sum' view of international relations.

The past decades have witnessed a diminishing degree of freedom in national policy-making. The need for economic policy coordination among the major actors of the international economy has grown. A number of international organizations exist to facilitate the increasing demand for cooperation. The demand of socialist countries for international policy cooperation has been marginal as long as they attributed only incidental functions to their extra-Comecon economic relations. For political and ideological reasons they remained aloof from the international institutional frameworks or were denied access for largely the same reasons. The changing perceptions and needs of socialist countries as well as the fact that they have become important actors in such global phenomena as the debt crisis, the ecological crisis, the security of

11. Clyde Farnesworth, "Study Finds Soviet Output is Stagnant," *The New York Times*, April 25, 1988, pp. D1–D2.

oil and commodity supplies and nuclear safety, have made their acceptance as partners in international multilateral policy coordination inevitable.

Practical Steps

The Soviet leadership seems to have realized that although the costs of adjustment and restructuring are substantial in a technologically changing world, the costs of remaining on the periphery of the global market economy are even greater. If *perestroika* is to succeed, heightened participation in the international economic system will be indispensable.

The Soviet Union has shown interest in encouraging increased East-West economic cooperation and integration. Ivan D. Ivanov, Deputy Chairman of the State Foreign Economic Commission of the USSR Council of Ministers, maintains that the restructuring of the economic mechanism also applies to foreign economic relations. This involves the deepening of socialist economic integration, supplementing trade relations with production-sharing and encompasses economic cooperation with capitalist and developing countries.[12] Soviet officials are actively exploring ways of normalizing trade with other countries to allow more flexibility for enterprises and organizations to engage in trade autonomously.[13]

The institutionalization of joint ventures and other forms of trade, finance and investment could enhance international security by creating a situation of greater predictability and mutual responsibility. Some of the Soviet proposals seem to signify more than a wish to seize short-term benefits to achieve tactical, political returns. They reflect strategic shifts away from long-held approaches that downplayed the importance of transnational processes and economic interdependence. If, in fact, this premise holds true, these shifts in attitude may be part

---

12. Interview with Ivan D. Ivanov, "On a Businesslike Basis: There Will Be Joint Enterprises," *Trud*, February 4, 1987, pp. 1-3, in *FBIS-SU*, February 12, 1987, pp. S1-S4.
13. Jozef M. van Brabant, *The GATT and Soviet Union: A Plea for Reform*, Working Paper No. 6, Department of International Economic and Social Affairs, United Nations, August 1987, p. 2.

of a long-term internal and external strategy based on redefined national interests.

There are a number of elements involved in the process of integration of the Soviet economy into the global economy. *Firstly,* the Soviet Union has expressed a desire to become more involved in international economic organizations, including GATT. Soviet officials claim that the ongoing reform nullifies the notion that the Soviet trade system and the GATT rules are incompatible.[14] Other officials refer to the ongoing accession of China to GATT as a precedent.[15] Naturally, the process of accommodation will take a long time, but this first step is an important political overture that would demonstrate to Western governments and potential business partners the seriousness of the opening up of the Soviet Union. As yet, there have been no official indications that the Soviet leadership is considering rapprochement with the main institutions of the international balance-of-payment and development-assistance regimes, i.e., the International Monetary Fund and the International Bank for Research and Development.

The Soviet Union should be aware that no immediate accession to these international bodies and thus no immediate benefits are likely to be possible. On the contrary, trading concessions for tactical short-run benefits may well be considered politically undesirable by the Soviet leadership. Moreover, the Soviet Union presumably wishes to enter these institutions as a developed country with considerable economic potential rather than as a country which needs to be bailed out, as has been argued in the West.

Secondly, the Soviet Union has passed a decree setting up a new form of economic cooperation with the West—the joint venture. The traditional Soviet strategy of purchasing turnkey plants from the West has proved to be expensive and of limited value without the constant input of Western technical and managerial expertise. The success of joint ventures will be seen

14. "Hopes for 'Positive' Response to GATT Request," TASS report (English), September 17, 1986, in *FBIS-SU,* September 19, 1986, p. CC3.
15. Mikhail Pankin, Ministry of Foreign Trade, USSR, quoted by Agence France-Presse, Paris, September 3, 1986, in *FBIS-SU,* September 4, 1986, p. CC4.

as an important litmus test regarding whether or not Soviet economic new thinking will have an impact in the global economy. The establishment of joint operations between the Soviet Union and Western companies can be seen as part of the process which could, in the long run, pave the way for the integration of the Soviet Union into the key international economic organizations. To date thirty-three joint venture agreements have been signed. Problems involved in the setting up of joint ventures (price formation and the convertibility of the ruble, for example) can be equated with similar problems which would accompany Soviet integration in GATT. Many foreign firms are frustrated by the slowness of decision-making and the lack of management expertise of their Soviet counterparts. The field of joint ventures can be explored both in strict economic terms and in terms of international security as well. The normalization of East-West economic cooperation through the framework of joint ventures can be viewed as a form of confidence-building measure and could over time contribute to security by helping each side to understand the other's policy environment.

Thirdly, the eventual conversion of the ruble has been discussed. As Academician Aganbegyan notes, senior Soviet officials envisage a three-tier conversion process—first involving domestic convertibility; second, convertibility among Comecon countries; and finally convertibility on the world market. Leonid Abalkin, Director of the Institute of Economics in Moscow, envisages the establishment of a convertible ruble perhaps in fifteen years. He identifies the following factors as sufficient to ensure that the Soviet economy will not be undermined through a freely convertible ruble and that convertibility is not the cause of domestic instability and further economic decline: the development of the machine-building industry so that products will be up to world standards; the reduction of grain purchases; and decisive improvements in the quality of consumer goods.[16] How clear a conception the Soviets have of the specific steps involved in such a process is still open to question.

Reforms in the Soviet Union and other East European coun-

---

16. "*Der Spiegel* Interviews Abalkin on Reforms," July 6, 1987, in *FBIS-SU*, July 10, 1987, pp. S1–S7.

tries could have significant political consequences for the general business environment of East-West relations and make Eastern economies structurally and logistically more responsive to the needs of international (and Western) markets. The reforms may facilitate Western access to a market of 400 million consumers at attractive geographical proximity to the main centers of Western economic power and help to solve current problems such as reciprocity in trade concessions, debates around trade practices and international financial transactions. But a cautionary note is needed here—there is no direct correlation between positive economic relations and a good political climate. The reverse is true as well. After the mid-1970s, for example, East-West economic relations began to worsen, yet the political climate improved. However, the formalization of economic links between East and West, founded on a solid economic basis, can engender trust, lessen suspicion and in the long run contribute to a more secure relationship.

Conclusion

There is a direct relationship between *perestroika* and economic security, both on a national and international level. Through a combination of administrative and economic measures discussed by Academician Aganbegyan and Professor Timofeyev in this volume, the Soviet leadership is seeking to modernize the domestic economy to meet the demands of the 1990s. On a global economic level, a move away from isolationism towards integration in the international economy is taking place and ground rules are being laid down for new forms of East-West economic cooperation. In the security field, the search for a more comprehensive approach to security is under way, moving away from a strictly military-oriented, unilateralist concept to a multidimensional understanding of the notion of collective security which integrates economic, social, humanitarian and military concerns. All of this presents a significant opportunity and challenge for the West. In order to take advantage of this situation, the West needs a clearer understanding of the reform debate within the Soviet Union. The following papers provide an important input for such a process.

Acceleration and Perestroika

by
Abel Aganbegyan

Editor's note:

During a series of discussions in New York and Moscow between IEWSS staff members and Academician Abel Aganbegyan in early 1988, a number of issues were raised concerning the process of restructuring currently taking place in the Soviet Union. There was considerable discussion about the Institute's bipartisan Task Force Report, How Should America Respond to Gorbachev's Challenge? *The following questions were among those which emerged from these discussions: How serious were the circumstances, described by General Secretary Gorbachev as "a pre-crisis situation," which led to the decision to launch a radical reform program? How substantial are the changes in the Soviet Union and what do they involve? What stage has the reform process now reached and what criteria will be used to judge its success? What is the interrelationship between social and economic factors? Are the changes in the national economy likely to facilitate an expansion of Soviet economic ties to the rest of the world?*

Academician Aganbegyan welcomed the Institute's Task Force Report and agreed to prepare a written response to major questions raised in the Report and in the subsequent discussions, in the hope that it would address "the lingering skepticism" in the West as to what perestroika *had achieved during its first three years.*

During recent meetings with specialists, government officials and business executives in the West, I became convinced of the need for Westerners to better understand the nature and purpose of *perestroika* and acceleration in the USSR. As is well known, a process of radical economic reform and restructuring (*perestroika*) is well underway in the Soviet Union. Even though we are faced with serious challenges, I believe this process will and must succeed. Measures have already been adopted to overcome the pre-crisis situation which existed in my country in the early 1980s. We have now entered a new stage of *perestroika*. Some see an inevitable contradiction between accelerating production and the satisfaction of social demands. Nonetheless, the outcome of *perestroika* depends specifically on the harmonious integration of social and scientific-technological development. This process is the core of the acceleration mechanism.

Why restructure? The old economic structure, the old economic policies, the management system and the old patterns of development did not correspond to the new conditions both inside the Soviet Union and internationally. From a position of relative strength, by the end of the 1960s both growth rates and social conditions in the health and housing sectors had begun to deteriorate in the Soviet Union. National income growth rates, for example, usually the most reliable indicator of national economic development, dropped 150 percent during the past fifteen years. The consequences of such a drop, and the economic stagnation it symbolizes, were very grave indeed; they well could have led to an exacerbated internal situation, fraught with serious social, economic and political crises. We should have halted these negative tendencies and worked out a program of "acceleration" much earlier. Instead, however, we continued in our set ways, automatically applying old methods without regard for the new conditions that had already begun to emerge.

What were these "new conditions"? Inside the Soviet Union, we had experienced a halt in the growth of all of our production resources—labor, raw materials, investments and assets. Major changes had taken place in the international marketplace. The scientific and technological revolution had entered a new stage. Unfortunately, in the 1970s and early 1980s we experienced a marked fall in production and labor-productivity growth rates; progress in the fields of science and technology had also slowed down. The role of man in the world economy had also changed. Yet we continued to hold to the so-called residual principle of distribution—allocating funds from the national budget into the social sphere only after insuring an increase in production.

In short, it became very clear that it was insufficient to make minor changes in the running of the economy. New, radical reform—a "restructuring"—was needed. This imperative was declared by the April 1985 plenary meeting of the Central Committee of the Communist Party of the Soviet Union (CPSU). The 27th CPSU Congress in February-March 1986 called for the formulation of policies which would lead to the acceleration of our social and economic development necessary to move away from stagnation.

The resultant program of restructuring is developing along three major lines. The first involves radical changes in the factors of economic development, and the structure of our national economy, in order for us to make the transition to the path of intensive development based on scientific and technological progress. The second involves turning our economy toward solving social tasks—that is, strengthening the social thrust of our development as a priority task. The third area entails radical reform in managing the whole mechanism of our national economy, without which neither the first nor the second effort can succeed.[1]

Restructuring is geared toward accomplishing our most important strategic task: the acceleration of the social and economic development of our country. In Western languages the words *perestroika* and *glasnost'* (openness) are already widely understood; yet the most important word of our economic strategy, *uskorenie*, or acceleration, has so far not gained wide circulation. In fact, the essence of the change is accelerating development.

The Growth Rate Problem

During the past fifteen years, our economy was operating with a noticeable decline in growth rates. In 1966–1970, the eighth five-year period, national income growth was 41 percent. In the ninth five-year period, it was 28 percent; in the tenth, 21 percent; and in the eleventh, only 16.5 percent. If we

1. I believe that the single most important statement to appear yet on the question of restructuring is the April 5, 1988, *Pravda* article, "Principles of Restructuring: Revolutionary Nature of Thinking and Acting." I have therefore requested that the Institute include the full text of this article as an appendix to this publication.

take into account that, during the eleventh five-year period, imports exceeded exports, the real growth of production was even smaller. Given the fact that our price indexes play down the real growth of prices, owing to incorrect methods of calculation, in reality we came to a situation of near-crisis stagnation in our economy during the eleventh five-year period. Our major task is to overcome those negative tendencies.

Restructuring is aimed at achieving this turnaround. In the twelfth five-year plan period, 1986–1990, we should increase our national income by as much as 22 percent. In subsequent five-year periods, we have to achieve a growth rate of 28 percent per period. But this quantitative aspect is not the most important factor in the concept of acceleration, if we understand it in a broader socioeconomic sense. The major factor in acceleration is the new *quality* of growth, that is, effecting changes in the sources of growth, intensification and social priorities mentioned above.

Let me briefly describe the existing problems and the possible ways to solve them. I will start with intensification. Economic growth can take place both through extensive factors (through an increment in resources), as well as through intensive factors (better use of those resources). During the last three five-year periods, the Soviet national economy was, for the most part, developing extensively. Our country is big, and of our 283 million residents, about 140 million are engaged in building the national economy. We cover one-sixth of the world's ground surface and have an abundance of natural resources. Each year we recover 2 to 3 billion tons of these resources, including 2.3 billion tons of fuel (as measured in coal equivalent). It was only natural for us to use those extensive resources, and in the process develop the country at their expense.

If one examines our typical five-year periods, say from the sixth through the ninth, we notice that our resources developed along the following lines. During each five-year period, major industrial assets grew by 50 to 60 percent, capital investments grew by 40 to 50 percent, and fuel and raw material production by 25 to 30 percent. At the same time, we were absorbing some 10 to 11 million workers into our economy.

According to optimization theory, we can estimate a universal indicator of resource consumption using efficiency coefficients measured in labor units. As I have calculated it, this indicator grew by 20 to 22 percent in the sixth through the eighth five-year periods. Beginning in the ninth five-year period, however, its growth slowed down. In the tenth five-year-plan period, the indicator growth rate dropped to 13 percent; in the eleventh, to 9 percent; and in the twelfth, to 7 percent. In the thirteenth and fourteenth five-year-plan periods, this figure will run at 5 and 6 percent, respectively.

How can one explain this drastic decline in growth rates? It is explained by the fact that we have reached a certain frontier in our development, when resources can no longer be expanded rapidly. In labor resources, we have run up against the demographic aftereffects of World War II. Those who were born during the war—and they totaled one-third of the prewar average for the same number of years—entered fertility twenty to twenty-five years after the war, and they gave birth to fewer children. Now their grandchildren are becoming part of the labor force. Thus, in the twelfth five-year-plan period, labor resources will increase by only 2.5 million people, compared with 10 to 11 million in the previous five-year periods. The majority of these 2.5 million young people will belong to the indigenous populations of Central Asia and Azerbaijan. Therefore, for the first time in our history, any increase in total output will have to be attained through greater labor productivity.

Let us turn to other resources, such as fuel and raw materials. The Soviet Union is the world's largest producer of oil, natural gas, iron ore and construction materials. We produce the same amount of timber as the United States, harvesting 2 million hectares of forest annually, and rank third in the world (after China and the United States) in coal production. Production rates, however, have been leveling off. In order to find and produce new raw materials and fuel, we have to go to remote areas and dig deeper into the soil, which costs more and more. New ecological requirements have made this method unprofitable. In the twelfth five-year-plan period, for the first time, two-thirds of our additional fuel requirements will be met through resource-saving measures. During subsequent five-year periods, this share will rise to between 75 and 80 percent. That is why we have to switch to conservation measures, and make resource-saving technologies more efficient.

We are also reducing the rate of growth of capital investments, along with fixed assets. For instance, in the ninth five-year-plan period, fixed assets grew by 53 percent; in the tenth, by 43 percent; in the eleventh, by 37 percent; and in the twelfth, they will increase by 30 percent.

Let us compare the figures for the last fifteen years with those for the next. Our national income grew by a factor of 1.8; in the future, we want to raise this growth factor to 2.0. But we want to achieve this with a smaller increment of resources. Fixed assets grew by a factor of three, and the output-capital ratio decreased. Over the next fifteen years, assets will double and the ratio will stabilize. In 1971–1985, fuel and raw material production grew by a factor of almost 1.5, while over the next fifteen years production will grow by a factor of 1.2, if that. The labor force engaged in material production grew by 15 percent over the last fifteen years, and in the next will grow by only 10 percent, due to the demographic aftereffects of the war and the increasing employment in the service sector.

Thus, we are counting on intensification to sustain growth. This means that we must accelerate the growth of labor productivity by a factor of 1.5, double our fuel savings, and overcome the low efficiency of investments and fixed assets. These measures will increase total economic efficiency by a factor of two and compensate for the decrease in resources, on the one hand, and impart the necessary acceleration, on the other.

When we know the growth of national income and the trend in resource-growth indicators, we are able to estimate growth in the general indicator of national economic efficiency, or what I would call "the indicator of intensification." During the last three five-year plans, this indicator grew by approximately 7 percent every five years, and that growth was very slow and marred by contradictions. Efficiency was growing, thanks to labor savings and some savings in fuel and raw materials. But those economies were partly lost because of capital-output ratio growth problems and the inefficient use of capital investments. These problems led to the slow growth of the general indicator. In the twelfth five-year plan we shall have to increase that efficiency indicator by 14 percent and by 21 percent in the five-year period thereafter. That will be real acceleration. And remember the complex nature of achieving those targets—namely, that we shall have to accelerate under conditions of lower resource-production levels.

The Social Sphere

In our country, there is a clearly visible gap between, on the one hand, the powerful potential of our state, its level of industrialization, the level of education of our population (secondary education is compulsory), and, on the other, people's living conditions. The lag in solving social problems is linked to the fact that, due to a series of objective reasons, resources had to be allocated to the development of heavy industry, to the strengthening of defense and the restoration of the economy which was destroyed during the war. The fall in the rates of economic growth with the manifestation of pre-crisis phenomena was especially felt in the social sphere, because the leadership decided to reallocate resources from the social sphere to the sphere of production. Addressing the social aspects of *perestroika* is an intrinsic part of the acceleration mechanism. It is time at last to understand that production is for the sake of the people, that the strengthening of social development has to be seen as the main aim of *perestroika*, for the people judge the course of *perestroika* above all by the change in their environment.

The most serious social problem is the shortage of housing. Seventeen percent of Soviet families do not have their own house or apartment; they live in hostels or two families share one apartment. We are building 2 million new apartments and houses a year. However, for a population of 283 million, this is not enough. Therefore, our task is to increase the rate of housing construction by a factor of 1.5 or more. This means 3 million new apartments a year. For the past twenty-five years, the average apartment size was designated as 105 square meters; now the average size is 130 square meters, which is a significant rise in living space. Moreover, since 1987, 12 million families a year are receiving new housing. In 1987 alone, 2.3 million new state apartments were built; 129 million square meters of living space were completed—17 million more than in 1985. The portion of capital investment designated for housing construction rose. According to our calculations, by the year 2000 every family will have either a comfortable apartment or a separate house. This requires considerable effort and serious work, including the attraction of people's savings. Rather than investing money in vodka, individuals are now being encouraged to invest in their own housing. In the past, local soviets controlled much of the building and allocation of housing, but now the share of cooperative and individual construction is increasing. It will have to continue to increase if we are to meet this fundamental priority.

Another acute problem is the food supply. Compared with other industrialized countries, we had several years ago a low-level consumption of meat products—sixty-two kilograms a year for each member of the population, vis-à-vis eighty-five kilograms in other countries. The Soviet Union also lags behind in the production of milk and dairy products in both variety and quality. In the Soviet Union, the population consumes less than half the medically prescribed norms of certain types of vegetables. It is very sad that a country as big as ours, with 80 percent of the world's black-soil areas, with diverse agroclimatic conditions, has to import grain and meat. True, we have arid and permafrost areas, but our fertile territories are tremendous.

The shortages are due to unsatisfactory management. Our task is to increase the growth rate of agricultural production by a factor of 2.5 and to increase the volume of production by 14.4 percent. To reach this goal, we have changed scientific research and investment policies; the entire existing system of agricultural management has been reorganized; and new agricultural management mechanisms have been introduced; emphasis has been placed on the spread of intensive technology; the family and collective contract system is becoming more widespread. Considerable sums have been allocated for the improvement of storage, preservation and processing facilities.

On the whole, these steps have yielded positive results. In 1987, in comparison with average annual production in previous five-year periods, we had a 30-million-ton increase in grain (from 180 to 210 million tons). Overall agricultural production in 1987 was 9 percent higher than that of previous years. We produced 2.7 million more tons of meat, 7 million more tons of milk, etc. These improvements allowed us to halve our imports of grain and meat. Today, the process of economic restructuring supports the growth of private plots and the individual ownership of dairy cows, which eliminates the need for such an infrastructure and facilitates the aforementioned tasks.

In order to balance demand and supply, we have to increase prices for meat and milk products. We have to change our retail pricing system. The existing prices for meat and milk were established in 1962. Since then, wages and salaries of collective farmers have grown. Milk and meat production is no longer profitable. Given the low retail price for meat in state shops, we give each Soviet customer a three-ruble subsidy every time he buys a kilo of meat. Similarly, we pay thirty kopeks in subsidy for every liter of milk sold. The subsidies for meat and milk alone amount to 57 billion rubles, with the state budget at only 430 billion rubles. Clearly, we do need to increase prices. But we recognize that large sectors of the population are wary of price increases. We want to handle this democratically, after making people aware of the problem through discussion, and with full compensation for the extra costs to be borne by the population.

Another problem is meeting the effective demand. We have a deformed structure of population expenditure patterns. Soviet taxes are very low (about 8 percent of nominal wages). Payment for apartments and utilities amounts to 3 percent of a typical household income. But because our system of services is not well developed, 80 percent of all expenditures goes to buy products. We have to change that structure through rapid development of the services sector. During the last five-year period, it grew by 25 percent, and this five-year period we have decided to increase it by 50 percent. Now we are planning to have an 80-percent increase for 1986–1990 and to adopt a series of measures, an entire program, to do it. The structure of people's expenditures will also shift with the wider voluntary use of personal savings for housing construction and other purposes.

Of course, it is very important to raise the quality of our manufactured goods to meet effective demand. This is why the economic management mechanism in light industry and trade was changed in 1986. We have scrapped centralized planning in these branches. The plan is now being formed through orders of trade that represent the demands of our population. Enterprises are reacting more flexibly to this change. We have also decentralized the retail price-setting that has been introduced for some new products and so-called bargain-price goods. The situation has improved a bit, but not to any considerable extent, because we need time to modernize light industry, equip it with new machines, and provide it with better raw materials.

Due to the low quality of consumer goods, an economic paradox exists. Although the volume of production is great, demand is not satisfied. For instance, this year we shall produce more than 800 million pairs of shoes—3.2 pairs per person. In Czechoslovakia, a country with a well-developed footwear industry, they produce 1.7 pairs of shoes per capita and this supply is enough. We produce two times as much, and do not meet the demand! Why? Because the quality is bad: the shoes are neither durable nor attractive. Thus, we need measures to improve quality. Together with the economic measures, we are implementing administrative ones. For instance, we introduced a state quality-control system in July 1986.

Concerning social issues, I could also mention the problem of pensioners or retired people. Because the Soviet Union lost 20 million people during World War II, and many more were wounded, many families lost their male breadwinners. Therefore, we have a huge number of pensioners: 57 million. The law on pensions adopted in 1956 is now out-of-date. A new law is being prepared that requires additional resources to raise pensions sufficiently. The retirement age is fifty-five for women and sixty for men, and there are five- or ten-year concessionary early-retirement periods for those working in the north or in harsh conditions.

A new, extended system of health services is being developed. Recognizing the importance of the health sector, the Soviet leadership has increased the medical budget 150 percent over the past two years. In addition, the salary of medical workers has risen by 30 percent (compared to the salary of other workers, whose salary has risen by 4 percent). In 1986, for the first time in twenty years, we managed to increase life expectancy by one year; it has now reached sixty-nine. This year it continues to rise. The problem of the high rate of infant mortality is being addressed; it is still high, but some improvements are visible. With respect to the problem of male mortality in the active years, the major scourge is alcoholism. Therefore, we decided to radically combat alcohol abuse with the introduction of the dry law in May 1985. In the last two years the purchase of alcoholic drinks has plunged by 50 percent. Accordingly, the male mortality rate has dropped rapidly. Now other measures are being taken to improve the level of health of our people, including a 40-percent growth of medical staff salaries (especially in the lower echelons of medicine).

In short, when Western analysts question the benefits of *perestroika* from the point of view of the consumer, they seem to look only at store shelves and to ignore the significant changes that are being introduced in many different social spheres. Questions of housing and health and heating and sanitation in schools are being seriously addressed. These areas dramatically affect the well-being of the population as a whole, and the well-being of the population directly affects the performance of the national economy.

Reforming the Mechanisms of Management

To solve the tasks of intensification and social development, the major preconditions are to restructure both the economy and economic management mechanisms. The basis of the administrative system is the command-ordering type of management—good for the barracks, for the military, for wartime or when a fire has to be put out, but not appropriate for peacetime, for managing scientific and technological revolutions, or when social and other requirements have grown and a transition is necessary from one set of methods of running the economy to another. We need to substitute economic for administrative methods. We want enterprises and associations to become self-accountable and self-financing. We want to enhance the self-governing role of labor collectives, including the elections of their managers and foremen. We want to establish a system of payment for labor that depends on the end-result of given activities for a given enterprise. But in order to achieve all this, we have to change the entire system of economic norms and standards, labor conditions and stimuli.

The major instrument of this radical reform will be a price

reform. We want to review wholesale and retail agricultural prices as well as retail prices. Later on, we will have to carry out a radical reform of our finance system to build a normative basis for all our enterprises. We want to change the credit and finance system and to align the money turnover with material turnover. All of this—new prices, a new credit system, a new finance system—will enable us to pass from a centralized distribution of the means of production (the so-called "material-supply system") to trade in the means of production. Customers will have some choice. This multi-channel trade presupposes a certain and considerable decentralization of prices. Although the state will control prices for key products and commodities to avoid inflation, other prices will be free or contractual. We also plan to prevent market monopolization by big enterprises.

These enterprises themselves will have to be changed. The interrelationship of supply, financing and pricing requires a thorough shake-up. Yet it will be difficult for us to move away from the direct, central allocation of capital goods to a system of wholesale buying and selling for the simple—ostensibly contradictory—reason that enterprises currently have too much money at their disposal. As soon as they would be allowed to buy what they please, the acquisitive instinct they have developed over the years would come into play, and they would increase stocks out of all proportion.

Such apprehensions are not simply speculation. A large-scale experiment conducted in 1984–1986 has shown that as soon as enterprises were given the go-ahead to make special purchases, they bought equipment and material for the "rainy days" ahead. The value of the stock in all of our enterprises exceeds 460 billion rubles—almost as much as the state's entire annual budget! Moreover, the stocks are growing twice as fast as production. Because enterprises acquired material resources largely by credit, there were years when enterprise production increased by 3 to 4 percent and debt by 10 to 15 percent. As a result, there is an enormous amount of spare money not geared to the real requirements of production. For this reason alone, the introduction of wholesale trade is necessary, and it must go hand-in-hand with the reform of finance and credit discussed at the 27th CPSU Congress.

Experience has shown that a price reform alone takes at least two years of preparation. But a lot of individual regulations and procedures can be changed without waiting for fundamental restructuring. In fact, some of the changes we seek to implement can only be achieved in waves. In industry, the first wave of restructuring is to introduce incentives in order to encourage fulfillment of contractual obligations to the greatest extent possible. The annual planning of wage funds allocated to individual enterprises has been abandoned for the establishment of long-term economic indicators. The second wave, which began in 1987, entails the transition to a self-financing system. Profit in self-financing becomes the main economic indicator, and a fixed percentage of profit (a long-term economic indicator) is all-important for management decisions. In 1987, self-financing was being practiced fully in five sectors of the economy, a number of large enterprises, the Soviet merchant marine industry, and in some sectors of trade. If this system proves its worth, it will soon predominate throughout our economy.

Finally, the third, most important wave of restructuring will be characterized by a radical expansion of the independence of individual enterprises. This wave, which requires careful preparation, will gain momentum only if the pricing system and the financial and credit mechanisms are also changed, when the transition to wholesale trade and trading between enterprises is completed. Then it will be possible to drastically reduce the number of old-type plan indicators, including those on the centrally planned list of products. It will be possible to do away with the present form of annual planning altogether and make the five-year plans a true target. When this third phase takes hold, there will be a supply and demand system, developing contractual relations not only horizontally, between enterprises, but also vertically. We will then be truly "managing" our economy.

Democratization, in the broadest sense, involving the active participation of the management and the workers in the economy, is a very important condition for the needed restructuring. This applies to the national economy, not only through enhancing the role of labor collectives and self-management, but through the establishment of cooperative bodies in trade, industry and the service sector. Many cooperatives have been concentrating their efforts on the fuller use of secondary supplies, industrial by-products and the manufacture of various items from them. In fact, at the beginning of 1988 more than 13,000 new cooperatives of this kind were in business. In all spheres our new law on individual labor encourages individual labor activity instead of prohibiting it. We are now in a transitional stage searching for new forms of labor activity. In due course an integrated program of private and state enterprise activity will be adopted.

Scientific and Technological Progress

The most important factor in *uskorenie,* strategically speaking, is to accelerate scientific and technological progress. In the past the results of scientific-technological research have unfortunately not taken root on a sufficiently wide basis. Such progress, as is known, involves two major processes. One is evolutionary—old technology or techniques are improved and updated but do not basically change. The other process is revolutionary—new generations of technological systems are invented to replace the old. Our country, until recently, has been developing predominantly along the evolutionary path of technological progress. We replaced equipment and goods very slowly, instead of scrapping the old technologies and products to develop new ones. Now we have changed our scientific and technological policy and decided to invoke revolutionary changes to modernize our economy.

The reasons for this are obvious. Take for example the "Zil" automobile, some features of which have been improved over the past twenty years. In principle the existing model has not changed. The same out-of-date car is still being produced even though the original model was not that good. Whereas car manufacturers in industrialized countries have significantly improved their models, we continue to produce the old ones. Likewise, I recently returned from Japan, where I visited Japan's most modern steel plant, constructed on man-made Ogishima Island near Yokohama. I was surprised to see the use of several patents that had been bought from the USSR. Those included patents for the dry extinguishing of coke, continuous casting and other techniques. The pioneer of continuous casting was our Novolipetsk steel plant. Japanese industry bought a license. Now 95 percent of Japanese steel is produced by this method, compared with only 30 percent of the steel produced in the USSR. Unfortunately, this example is typical.

Thus, the major problem is to implement our achievements in science and technology by insuring their widespread diffusion. The implementation of a technology is materialized through new equipment, machines and instruments. It means that machine-building—the sector where such equipment and machines are produced—is the key to our plans for diffusion.

Our machine-building (civilian machine-building) is a very backward industry. In light of modern requirements it is obsolete. Because it does not provide other industries with new equipment, we are lagging behind in all areas affected by this backwardness. That is why we have proclaimed, and are now implementing, a new overall investment policy. The essence of it is to redistribute resources in favor of machine-building. To cite just a few figures, during the last five-year-plan period capital investments in machine-building grew by 24 percent. In the current five-year plan we intend to have an 80-percent increase. In 1986–1987 alone, the volume of capital investment in the machine-building industry increased by 50 percent, i.e., more than during the entire eleventh five-year plan. Despite the fact that this increase in investment has yet to show itself fully in the renewal rate of machine-building-industry products, we have done more during the past two years than in the previous five. But we are going to do even more. In the last five-year-plan period, we threw away only 9 percent of the machines and equipment from our active plants, leaving over 90 percent of the aging assets remaining. Now in the twelfth five-year plan, we plan to renew 45 percent of them. To provide for this modernization, we are going to increase machine tools production by a factor of four and purchase new equipment from abroad. We have started working the newer machines over two or three shifts, while the old machines are working only 1.3 shifts.

To transform the technological basis of our machine-building industry, we are changing the output structure. We have to renew three-fourths of our machine-building production in the near future—in the next six years. In 1985 the rate of renovation of our civilian machine-building production was 3.1 percent. In 1987, that figure had not grown much—to 9 percent. We are now rapidly increasing that material basis so that, in 1987, the annual renovation rate will have been 7.5 percent, and by 1990, 13 percent. In the twelfth five-year plan as a whole, we seek to have half of our machine-building output replaced with new products. This new equipment will be 1.5 to two times more productive, with doubled reliability, and 12 to 18 percent less costly in terms of metal consumption.

The idea is to reconstruct our machine-building industry and accelerate its rate of development so that it grows two times faster, and new research-and-development-intensive industries three to four times faster, than our national economy as a whole. Machine-building is the foundation for the technical reconstruction of all areas of the economy. If we look at equipment and machines, we notice that the rate of renovation is 3 percent per year, and we want to increase this to 6.2 percent. Of course, quite a number of difficulties exist, and we feel them as one would feel fetters—old projects, old designs, old fixed-capital assets and old organization of labor. Although the momentum is beginning to build, we recognize the serious difficulties that will have to be overcome.

The development of all areas of production also depends on advances in engineering, especially electronics and instrument-making. Engineering is a priority precisely because new technologies and new inventions can be tested only through engineering. Our scientists are criticized for the extremely slow rate at which their inventions are being introduced into the national economy and diffused. More often than not this is the fault of engineering. Studies have shown that 71 percent of serial engineering output does not correspond to modern requirements. In machine-tool construction and instrument-making 86 percent and 83 percent of output, respectively, are below world standards. The USSR is suffering serious losses which can no longer be sustained. It is necessary now to halt certain production lines and replace them with more modern ones. Only 3.1 percent of all engineering products were modernized in 1985; now we are aiming to raise this figure to 13 percent.

Because of the importance of engineering, we plan to increase investment in it by 80 percent in the present five-year plan, as compared to a mere 30 percent in the previous five-year plan. Engineering is to receive unprecedented funding for development—63 billion rubles over the next five years—and these funds must be used wisely. In effect, by 1990 almost 60 percent of the technical base in engineering is to be renewed. The production of machinery will also have to meet a very high target: by 1990, 80 to 95 percent of all products will have to measure up to the highest standards in the world. As we replace old equipment, productivity must rise 1.5 times, and reliability double. The consumption of metal per unit of product, as noted above, is to be reduced by 12 to 18 percent. Many reconstruction plans have to be redrawn with this in mind.

International Economic Relations

All of these changes in the national economy will be called upon to facilitate the expansion of our foreign economic ties. We have in mind, in particular, to increase the influence of financial and credit levers. We will adopt effective measures in order to improve our import-export structure and broaden cooperation in production. Moreover, we are directing our attention to the issue of the ruble's convertibility, so that it can be introduced in stages. First we plan to introduce domestic convertibility, followed by convertibility on the international socialist market, that is, within the Council on Mutual and Economic Assistance (Comecon). The third stage would come in the 1990s, when we plan to introduce it on the world market.

The first steps in institutional reform have already been taken. The right of trading internationally in the free market has been given to twenty ministries, whereas previously it was the monopoly of the Ministry for Foreign Trade. Over seventy enterprises and trusts have been granted the right to go into international markets and to create special foreign trade firms. About 1,000 enterprises were given the right to trade with socialist countries in the socialist world market. Soon, in 1989–1990, price reforms will take place, taking into account world prices. This will facilitate our introduction of the convertible ruble.

As we move toward a more open economy and extend our foreign economic relations faster than our economy is growing, we must learn how to produce high-quality goods. We want to sell not only raw materials and fuel, but ready-made articles as well. We have also decided to embark on a joint-venture system, and we have already received about 400 inquiries that are being considered. The first thirty-three joint ventures (as of April 1988) have already been created.

We are against autarky. Thus, we are now playing an active role in the work of a number of international economic fora. In addition, we feel it is important to eliminate the inadequacies of present-day economic relations, such as discrimination or limitations in trade and economic relations and the absence of Soviet membership in the General Agreement on Tariffs and Trade (GATT) and other organizations. The Soviet Union is taking part in the development of a comprehensive system of international security by strengthening international economic security. It was at the Soviet Union's initiative that the United Nations General Assembly adopted the resolution stating that international economic security comes from the necessity to secure favorable foreign conditions for socioeconomic development in all countries of the world. In the present environment, in which we seek international stability, economic cooperation has a special significance. In particular, tremendous potential exists for the broadening of multilateral and bilateral Soviet-American economic cooperation. Mikhail Gorbachev spoke precisely and repeatedly on this point when he met with prominent representatives of the U.S. business community during his visit to Washington in December 1987. "Economic cooperation and trade between our two countries," he said, "is one of the factors in domestic development and for a more stable international situation."

Conclusion

After the April 1985 CPSU Central Committee plenary session, we elaborated a new system of management, an economic management mechanism. At the June 1987 plenary session it was adopted. At the following session of the Supreme Soviet, a new law for state enterprises, declaring their independence as a basic element of the new management system, was accepted. Later the CPSU Central Committee and the Council of Ministers decreed new steps in this direction: the restructuring of planning, price-setting, finance, banking, material supply, regional governing, labor and social affairs, statistical systems, etc.

Thus in our country we have started a full-scale transition from verbal declarations to the creation of a new management system, from isolated experiments to the wide diffusion of new approaches, all aimed at real economic reform. A schedule for this transition, by which the new economic management system will come into force during the next, the thirteenth, five-year-plan period, has already been developed.

For economists it is a very interesting time to live in the Soviet Union. Now that society has started moving, we see people in action—reading newspapers and actively debating, criticizing and discussing what is written, for example—and feeling that their lives are becoming easier. Now the challenge is to achieve better living conditions and greater labor productivity while retaining our vital and interesting spiritual life. Striking a balance between the radical reform process and the objective of securing domestic economic growth, in the framework of a stable but flexible international security system, is the focus of the *uskorenie* in the Soviet Union today. Indeed, the restructuring process underway in my country is real and not cosmetic and it will move forward.

Social Aspects of Perestroika

by
Timor Timofeyev

Editor's note:

During discussions in New York and Moscow betweeen IEWSS staff and Professor Timor Timofeyev, Director of the Institute of International Labor Studies, the following questions on the social, cultural and political aspects of the reform process were raised. How has perestroika *already affected the lives of the workers? In what ways has worker participation increased in the course of the reform? How will the leadership strike a balance between efficiency and equity in the reform process? Will unemployment play a role? Is it possible to integrate elements of the market mechanism in the centrally planned economy? Professor Timofeyev addressed these questions in the following paper.*

In 1988 the process of restructuring in the Soviet Union—known to the West by the name *perestroika*—entered a new, second stage. Between 1985 and 1988, the Soviet Union developed the integral concept of restructuring, substantiated it theoretically and politically, and created the domestic and international atmosphere necessary for achieving *perestroika*'s objectives. In 1988, the radical economic reform began to be broadly implemented in practice. The democratization of public life has further developed, and the participation of the Soviet people in the process of reform has increased.

General Secretary of the Communist Party of the Soviet Union (CPSU) Mikhail Gorbachev specifically noted in January 1988 that the USSR had completed the first stage of *perestroika* and entered the second stage.[1] It became clear during

1. "Democratization—the Essence of *Perestroika*, of Socialism. Meeting with Ideological Workers and Heads of the Mass Media in the CPSU Central Committee," *Pravda*, January 13, 1988.

the first stage what needed to be done and how to go about doing it. Now the most complex stage has begun, when the concept of *perestroika* must enter the lives of millions of Soviet people. That which had been realized by the political leadership, by the advanced strata of our people, should now be realized by the public at large. These challenges of further developing democratization in the country and the Communist Party will be given special attention at the special 19th All-Union Conference of the CPSU, slated to take place at the end of June 1988.

Democratization

In this light, outside observers looking in should focus their attention on *two elements* of the radical economic reform now being implemented. One is the growing *economic independence of enterprises.* As a result of this increasing independence, enterprises are independently developing plans for economic and social growth. Both the five-year and the annual plans which used to control enterprise activity are now, for the most part, recommendations. State "orders" remain obligatory, but their impact will gradually diminish as all enterprises more broadly utilize independent economic links. In short, interference from above (i.e., from ministries) is diminishing and in principle will cease to affect enterprise operations. The influence on enterprise activity will become mostly economic, not administrative.

The second element, directly connected to the first, is the *real increase in the role of labor collectives,* which also means the expansion of worker participation in the consideration and solution of all major economic and social problems. In accordance with the new Soviet law on the state enterprise (which entered into force in January 1988), labor collectives will earn their own income, and, with the help of new economic levers such as the system of profit and loss, will be responsible for all economic and financial aspects of enterprise activity. The more efficient the work, the greater will be the collective's income. The collective will elect enterprise managers, approve the plan of its economic and social development and collective contract, and adopt internal labor regulations. The labor collective, not some administrative organ above it, will determine how best to use its own development funds, how and when to pay workers, how to distribute housing and day-care, how to pay out bonuses and other benefits, and so on. The labor collective will thus increasingly become the master of the enterprise. The labor-collective soviets (councils) will constantly function as organs of self-management, and their role will help to expand enterprise rights and contribute to the process of reform.

Admittedly, there has been a certain time lag between the implementation of *perestroika* measures and changes in the production conditions and workers' living standards. So far we have failed to solve our housing and food problems, saturate the market with consumer goods, resolutely increase the supply of services, especially health services, and so on. Although one might conclude from this delay that the influence of *perestroika* is small, this is clearly not the case. *Perestroika*'s effect on *glasnost'*, freedom of opinion and freedom of the press has been obvious. Its range affects many areas of cultural, social, political and economic life. The process of *perestroika* in the economy has only just begun, and its speed today is affected by earlier years of slow economic development and static social policies. Further, not all enterprises have been switched to new conditions of economic management. Moreover, differences between the personal interests of individual social groups and the fundamental interests of a society as a whole frequently occur in social and political life; and they have been manifest in our country. In his new book *Perestroika*, published in the West in late 1987, Soviet General Secretary Mikhail Gorbachev directly addresses this divergence between the fundamental interests of society, the vanguard of which is ready for large-scale changes, and the momentary, vested interests of certain people.[2]

The Human Factor

As we pursue our strategy of "acceleration" (*uskorenie*) by ensuring economic, scientific and technological progress, the

2. Mikhail S. Gorbachev, *Perestroika: New Thinking for Our Country and the World* (New York: Harper and Row, 1987).

social, political, philosophical and moral aspects of *perestroika* also receive our attention. Yet some people in the West either underestimate or purposely ignore the social aspect of *perestroika*. Devoting their attention solely to the economic and technological aspects of Soviet reform, many outside observers fail to appreciate the connection between economic processes and their effect on politics, science and research. Most observers have not recognized that in contemporary socialist society, reform is actually aimed at increasing the human factor, humanizing, in a word, all social, including international, relations.

This attention to the human factor permeates all of our current national programs of development and is expressed in concrete social programs directed at the solution of existing problems. The legislation which provides the basis for the radical reform of our economy—the Law on the State Enterprise (June 1987), the Law on Individual Labor Activity (November 1986) and others—bridge the twin objectives of economic and social development. Moreover, as this legislation has been implemented a number of programs have been adopted which are directly aimed at solving social problems such as health care and housing. Proposals for improving our educational system were debated at the Central Committee plenary meeting of February 1988. We have also focused on the solution of acute environmental problems, as indicated, for example, by our decision to rebuild the industrial enterprises which pollute Lake Baikal and Lake Ladoga. Actions addressed at social ills have been put into effect, such as the anti-alcoholism campaign.

Programs aimed at increasing the rate and improving the quality of production are by their very nature part of the solution of social problems. True, the introduction of payment based on enterprise self-sufficiency means the liquidation of the egalitarian elements of income distribution that were blind to the quantity and quality of the work performed. But a system of remuneration based on the principle of payment according to worker contribution improves the social climate.

Perestroika takes into account the human factor by seeking to strike a balance between efficiency—one of its highest-priority objectives—and equity. Achieving a higher rate of labor efficiency is dependent not only on deeper differentiation in remuneration, but on a more general type of differentiation. In the economic conditions created by radical reform, a worker's income will depend not only on the result of work in state enterprises, but also on cooperative and individual labor activities. Obviously, the system of labor remuneration that has existed in the Soviet Union since the early 1930s—when an efficient and a less efficient worker earned just about the same—has shaped over the intervening decades a social consciousness here that has interpreted wage-leveling as social justice. Therefore, one can assume that changes in both the size and type of wage differentiation will not be welcomed by all sectors of the population. Sizeable categories of workers exist whose level of training, age, ability and physical conditions make them unprepared for intensive labor, complex, responsible positions, or even efficient work. It goes without saying that these categories of people will interpret the new type of differentiation as a breach of social justice. New problems and conflict situations may arise—ones which society is not yet ready to resolve. The stream of "Letters to the Editor" in our newspapers attests to the depth of the leveling tendencies in our social consciousness—tendencies which are increasingly manifest as new cooperative and individual labor activities keep bringing in high earnings.

New Theoretical Approaches

In order to redress what was neglected in the past, it is necessary to address directly a number of serious errors which were committed. In this spirit, it was stated frankly at the January 1987 plenary meeting of the CPSU Central Committee that the former leadership of the country failed to fully appreciate the urgent necessity for change. It did not recognize the dangers stemming from growing stagnation. Furthermore, it failed to rise to the challenge—and the challenge still exists—of successfully utilizing the full creative potential of socialism. In various spheres of Soviet life, including, importantly, social theory, inertia predominated, along with a desire to ignore all things that did not fit into traditional patterns of understanding. The dialectics of socialism's contradictions—in a word, the actual situation of our society—was not a subject of study. For several decades Soviet theorists proceeded from the belief that everything about socialism, especially its economic mechanism, had emerged, and required no alteration, from the ideas of the 1920s and 1930s. Socialism, however, like any other social system, is subject to constant transformation and should be so interpreted.

Indeed, changes in the structure of Soviet society in the 1960s and 1970s *necessitated* a rethinking of economic and social policies. The most important change is the general growth of the educational and training standards of the entire working class. At the end of the 1970s the share of workers who had completed secondary education had increased fivefold from the 1950s. From the mid-1960s to the early 1980s, the number of workers with a high level of industrial training increased by a factor of 1.5. The number—both in absolute and relative terms—of people whose jobs are related to the scientific-industrial sector of the economy has steadily increased. Unfortunately, the development of such complex, dynamic production has been hindered by excessively administrative, centralized management. The fact that Soviet workers in the scientific-industrial sphere have become a sector unto themselves, constituting one-sixth of all industrial workers, has necessitated the transition to a flexible system of management, an expansion of the independence of economic units, and the consolidation of democratic principles in production.

At the same time, significant changes have taken place in the social outlook of the workers employed in traditional industrial production. (These workers currently represent over half of our employed population and over 60 percent of our industrial workforce.) The growth of their educational standards and culture has contributed to the formation in their mass consciousness of ideas about the inadequacy of the existing order of things. In a word, they have increased expectations. They, as well as their countrymen, are aware that our national economy, which lacked elements of producer independence, was dominated in parts by rigid centralization, and corresponded to the needs of development in particular sectors, rather than the requirements of truly balanced growth.

As we introduce greater clarity into the study of Soviet societal development—especially of the role of working people and their organizations—we have to be careful to avoid two dangerous tendencies: 1) to justify phenomena of stagnation, and 2) to design far-reaching reform without first constructing a proper foundation for it. In social theory, it is necessary to study the dynamic relationship between the productive forces and the modes of production. For here lie some of the key problems in our strategy of acceleration. One cannot consider economic reform only from the viewpoint of restructuring the management mechanisms. One has to study questions of getting workers more interested in the optimum development of productive forces, and questions of realizing the potential of all forms of socialist ownership. In addition, it is important to search explicitly for methods of increasing the role of the "human factor" as a means of realizing the objectives of reform. The experience gained from new trends of self-management and elections at enterprises is of great importance for those concerned with expanding the role of the working class in production. The various forms of social and political activity of the working class, and the restructuring of the work of party and trade union organizations, deserve close study in the future. It is also necessary to understand the social consequences of economic reforms, and, consequently, how to formulate social policy directed at increasing labor efficiency.

Social scientists in the Soviet Union are presently engaged in the most lively and interesting theoretical discussions. Many of them touch upon fundamental and complex problems that have not been adequately explored and debated in our society. Others are concerned more with the continuing development of a number of subjects which had been debated in the past. These problems include the same issues being confronted in practice: the relationship between the centrally planned economy and market under socialism; the relationship between productive and non-productive labor; the relationship of various forms of ownership under socialism; the character of structural changes in the economy caused by the scientific and technological revolution; and trends and prospects in the development of the working class, especially professional groups, under the new conditions of restructuring.[3] A great deal of attention is also being paid to the causes of the "deceleration mechanism" and methods to overcome them.

Employment Changes and Market Mechanisms

One question under study, for example, is the role of employment changes in reform. Full employment has been a fundamental tenet of Soviet society since 1930. Of course we would like to avoid mass unemployment as we implement economic reform. Even though we did away with unemployment in 1930, the number of people who wanted to work and the number of people who had jobs never corresponded completely. Such contradictions have usually had a temporary and local character, and more often than not it was connected with a labor shortage. Today, as we render the Soviet economy increasingly efficient, the number of available jobs will be pared down, and the search for work will become more intense. On the one hand, our economy will have ample opportunities for ensuring work for the mass of the able-bodied population: the greater efficiency of equipment use, the development of the service sphere, the expansion of the network of small enterprises producing consumer goods all will secure this. On the other hand, governmental and planning organs are already preparing solutions for the problem of the mass release of workers and employees from high-technology production that is coming under the new (profit-and-loss) system of economic management. This particular question was debated and included in the recent decision of the CPSU Central Committee and the USSR Council of Ministers, which, among other measures, envisaged material assistance to such workers during the period in which they are looking for new jobs. Measures taken by the Soviet leadership at the February 1988 plenary meeting of the Central Committee—mapping out

3. See, for example, "On the Essence of the Deceleration Mechanism" (discussion) in *Problemy istorii KPSS* (Problems of History of the CPSU) 1 (1988), pp. 128–134; also *The Working Class and Contemporary World* No. 2 (1988), pp. 3–11, 42–57.

programs for qualitative improvements in the levels of education and vocational training for young people—are aimed at the solution of this problem as well.

Another question concerns methods of integrating elements of market mechanisms with mechanisms of planning. Without integrated market mechanisms, a planned economy loses efficiency and finds it difficult to progress along the road to economic development. (Likewise, an unlimited market economy with absolutely no planning mechanisms results in social and economic catastrophe.) One has to keep in mind that in the framework of such integration the nature both of the market mechanism and planning changes drastically. Centralized planning using the market mechanism is not the same centralized planning that evolved in the Soviet Union during the 1930s and 1940s and which retains its major features even today. Certainly, attempts to integrate this kind of planning with market mechanisms are hopeless. But stimulatory price planning, indirectly regulated, which resorts to economic levers can efficiently implement the goals of society.

Education Reform

Issues of education reform have also begun to take a larger place in scientific research, as evidenced by the February 1988 CPSU Central Committee plenum. Improvements in the Soviet educational system must take into account one of the most interesting trends in contemporary culture: that toward continuing education. This includes the primary schooling and vocational training of the young before they begin working, as well as the retraining which often takes place later in life. The contemporary trend toward continuing education has been determined by fundamental shifts in the means of production, foremost among them the ever-shortening duration of major technologies and the professions associated with them. Clearly, a comprehensive study of the requirements of contemporary high technology for worker training is very much needed. The changes necessary for vocational training should be studied in a new light—namely that, as a general rule, the introduction of new technologies makes it necessary to supplement general education with systematic vocational training. Finally, in these studies of continuing vocational education, it will be important to take a look at the steps other countries have been taking.

Such international perspectives will help us to raise the level of Soviet worker consciousness on the threshold of the twenty-first century.

We have also developed comparative research programs, studying the labor movements in various countries. A number of scientific conferences devoted, for example, to political and economic problems of capitalism, to new phenomena in international relations and the development of the world revolutionary process have recently been convened. Among the new works by Soviet scholars one should point out the monograph *Capitalism at the Close of the Century,* edited by Alexander Yakovlev. This book analyzes the main contradictions of the world capitalist system, the urgent problems of international security in our time and the significance of new political thinking for the survival of mankind.[4] Let us also note a new collective work on the development and struggle of the working class, prepared by the Institute of International Labor Studies of the USSR Academy of Sciences for the centenary of May Day. On the basis of the history of the international revolutionary experience and the lessons of the workers' organizations (from the emergence of the proletarian movement to the present period), this study emphasizes that the dynamism of the working class is one of the main sources of its strength, and that this dynamism remains the most important condition for success in the implementation of the working class's future social role.[5]

The structure of the contemporary labor force is changing significantly. Some Western authors maintain that the "erosion" of the working class is taking place, and repeatedly refer to the "lack of any prospect" for the working-class movement. To some extent these ideas have an influence on some left-radical researchers of social problems, who have even begun to lobby for abandoning the very term "working class."

---

4. See Alexander Yakovlev, ed., *Capitalism at the Close of the Century,* (Moscow: 1987).
5. A. Galkin, T. Timofeyev and A. Chernayev, eds., *The Working Class and World Development: Stages of Struggle* (Moscow: Mysl', 1987).

Marxists, it goes without saying, do not deny that important changes—qualitative and quantitative—are taking place in the ranks of the working class. The number of workers with new professions continues to increase. In recent decades the world's labor force has grown to almost 700 million people, compared to 117 million at the beginning of the 1920s. The ranks of the working class in socialist countries are increasing rapidly. Their number has already exceeded 200 million. When analyzing trends in the development of the working class in socialist society, the working class, we believe, is the main social force. Powerful changes have taken place in its composition and social outlook; not only its numerical strength, but also the level of its professional skills, education and culture have grown. The new ranks of the labor force are reinforced more and more by highly skilled workers—by "mental" labor even more than by manual. Moreover, as noted above, today's working class has increased expectations.[6] The working class, which represents, in number, the predominant force in society, has the potential to play a decisive role, particularly at historical turning-points.[7] It is not accidental, therefore, that the way working people participate in *perestroika* has attracted so much attention.

Political and Cultural Dimensions

In contrast to those who interpret *perestroika* from a technocratic point of view, Marxists proceed from the assumption that it needs to be studied—and, ultimately, judged—from all angles. A truly scientific study of *perestroika* should therefore use a multidisciplinary approach. Not only is creativity now required in the disciplines of political economy, sociology, political science, philosophy and law, but in the hard and

---

6. See, for example, *Some Tendencies and Problems in the Development of the Working Class* (Moscow: Institute of International Labor Studies of the USSR Academy of Sciences); Anatoly Dobrynin, "Major Social Force of Our Times," *Obschchestvennye nauki* (Social Sciences) (Moscow) 18, No. 3 (1987), pp. 8–21.
7. Mikhail S. Gorbachev, "October and Perestroika: the Revolution Continues" (Report at the Jubilee Meeting in the Kremlin, November 2, 1987).

natural sciences as well. Today, numerous interdisciplinary groups of Soviet scientists are studying major international problems, the principles of new political and economic thinking, the development of various kinds of ecological studies (including various civic initiatives in this sphere)[8] and changes in social consciousness. Thus when we refer to the necessity for adopting a broad approach to complex social phenomena, we are referring to both theory and practice.

A key political aim of the second stage of *perestroika* is the more energetic involvement of the Soviet people in various forms of political activity. This both facilitates and benefits from the diffusion of democratization processes among various levels of social life. It also demands the extension of *glasnost'* in the work of state and local organizations. A series of measures directed at developing the legal framework for the active involvement of workers in the political process is being developed. The evolution of new legal norms, as well as the revision of existing laws, is significantly increasing the rights and opportunities of the population to participate in the decision-making process. At the same time, new actions are being implemented in order to elect management—in various bodies, but especially industry—based on the principle of choice between several candidates.

The increased popular activity in political life promotes the emergence of numerous social movements, organizations and foundations. This is demonstrated by the organization of women's movements and war veterans. Such organizations as the Environment Foundation, Children's Foundation, the Soviet Foundation of Culture and others have acquired considerable social influence. Using voluntary contributions these organizations have spirited along the political and social activity in our country.

The activity of various single-issue initiative groups is also on the rise. Their actions have helped, for example, in stopping the project to direct our northern rivers into the Caspian Sea, slowed industrial damage to the Irkutsk River, and prevented the destruction of various architectural landmarks—all of which has contributed in various ways to social development. Such organizations as the Union of Soviet Writers, the Union

8. See, for example, the issue of *Obshchestvennye nauki* 18, No. 3, p. 71.

of Filmmakers and the Union of Theater Workers (a new organization) have begun to involve themselves more energetically in social issues. Last but not least, the new open dialogue with leaders at various levels, including the mass media, about the means of production, is now affording the public an excellent means for controlling the work of all economic organizations.

International Affairs

In our rapidly changing world, the links between national and international processes are growing stronger. In fact, in the nuclear age, international and national security have become particularly interconnected. "Interdependence" describes—in our contradictory world—international life better than at any other time in the past. With this in mind, we look at our restructuring program—its economic and political aspects—in both domestic and international terms. *Perestroika,* as we see it, relates to more than just Soviet life. The world as a whole could use a restructuring, considering the fact that it is saturated with nuclear weapons and beset with serious economic and ecological problems. Thus, one can speak of the need for a *perestroika* of international relations.

New Soviet foreign policy initiatives have been accompanied by considerable changes in the style of our diplomacy. Flexibility is one of the typical features of our new political thinking. This is specifically demonstrated by the Soviet-American arms control negotiations and the efforts of the USSR to achieve an agreement on the liquidation of medium- and shorter-range missiles. The efforts to work out the Soviet-American agreement on the 50-percent reduction of strategic weapons and the comprehensive nuclear test ban are also of great significance.

Efforts to provide for the participation of the public in order to develop cooperation between peoples of the world is helping to improve the climate of confidence. The role of mass organizations which present various initiatives directed at mutual understanding between peoples and overcoming enemy images has become an integral part of international efforts to consolidate neighborly relations.

If the world community accepts the responsibility that interdependence mandates for all of its members, then serious joint efforts are necessary. The United Nations, for example, has great potential for strengthening peace and international security, but joint efforts on the part of the entire world community are needed in order to realize it. This idea has been repeatedly developed by Soviet leaders. In an address to the UN General Assembly, Gorbachev declared that the main objective of the UN Charter has still not been achieved—there are, as yet, no guarantees of stable peace.

The principles of new political thinking for international relations are based not on temporary or self-serving considerations, but on a deeply-rooted philosophical foundation. CPSU official documents proclaim that the dialectics of contemporary development consist of 1) competition between the two systems, and 2) a growing tendency towards international interdependence. This is how Soviet people see the present world—full of controversy, but interdependent, and in many ways an integral whole. This view of the global problems facing mankind increasingly finds expression in the works of a number of Soviet specialists in the political, economic, philosophical and other sciences.

New political thinking is useful in the analysis of international conflicts. All scholars recognize the relevance of the topic for current affairs. But some in the West are pessimistic about the value of studies that examine the deep-rooted causes of various conflicts—studies that reveal their interconnections, effectively investigate their topology and search for means of resolution. Some people still underestimate the dangers posed by regional conflict.

Likewise, the dangers of nuclear weapons have still not been fully understood. In the years after the nuclear explosion at Hiroshima, not only Albert Einstein and Bertrand Russell, but military leaders such as Douglas MacArthur and Dwight Eisenhower recognized the suicidal nature of nuclear-weapons use, and the danger of allowing them to become the basis of defense postures and an instrument of international competition. These men and others called for "the adoption of a new mindset—a new way of looking at things, one based on the recognition that war was no longer a rational option for great industrial powers and that other means would have to be found to resolve the conflicts of interest that would always be bound to arise among them."[9] They spoke with a sense of urgency, hoping that their warnings would not fall on deaf ears, that a new generation of leaders would recognize the existence of these new political realities.

Alas, this has not happened. As George F. Kennan points out, their warnings have been ignored in many respects by influential circles in the West. There has been no "new mindset." There has been no recognition of the uniqueness of the weapons of mass destruction, no recognition of the dangers inherent in their uncontrolled development. On the contrary, nuclear explosives have come to be treated as just another weapon, vastly superior to others, of course, in the capacity for indiscriminate destruction, but subject to the pre-nuclear-age assumption that "the value of a weapon is simply proportionate to its destructiveness and that the more you have of any weapons, in relation to similar holdings of your adversary, the more secure you are. . . ."[10]

How does the Soviet leadership approach these issues? In a chapter written for a new book, *The Basics of Diplomacy*, Anatoly Kovalev (First Deputy Foreign Minister of the USSR) notes that regional conflicts historically have escalated, even broken out, as a result of the interference, and sometimes direct armed intervention, of outside forces. Imperialist actions have involved the bayonets of the marines, soldiers of "rapid deployment" forces and occasionally mercenaries. But at the same time, Kovalev urges his readers not to overlook the accumulated contradictions around the world. Thus, arbitrary proclamation of zones of "vital interests" and the policy of "neo-globalism" generally lie at the root of conflict, but they do not exclude problems of vestigial colonialism, national and religious beliefs, and competing domestic institutions, parties, sects and people. It would be wrong to forget that such "homemade fuel" is capable of spontaneous combustion.

The approach of the Soviet Union lies in disengaging from conflict situations where they exist, in implementing preventive measures aimed at avoiding "spontaneous combustion,"

9. George F. Kennan, "Foreword," in Norman Cousins, *The Pathology of Power* (New York: W. W. Norton, 1987), p. 9.
10. Ibid., p. 10.

and, what is more, in checking the temptation for military adventures in regions fraught with the danger of explosion. Regional conflicts in fact should not be a zone of rivalry between two or more large powers. A cautious, responsible approach to these problems, and not the policy of brute force and constant threats, is the only realistic one. The Soviet Union proposes to other parties to act jointly in the search for conflict resolution.

Conclusion

The restructuring of both Soviet life and international relations confronts numerous obstacles, including subjective ones. The pressure of old stereotypes of thinking works like a braking mechanism. In addition, numerous objective complexities require solution for contradictions in national and international life to be resolved. And it is true that, measured against what remains to be done, very little has been accomplished so far. But the first signs of change are evident. Entering this second stage of *perestroika*, the Soviet leadership is optimistic about the future.

Appendix

"Principles of Restructuring: Revolutionary Nature of Thinking and Acting," Pravda, *April 5, 1988, p. 2 (edited translation of the Foreign Broadcast Information Service-SU,* National Affairs, *April 5, 1988, pp. 37–43).*

The April 1985 plenum of the CPSU Central Committee initiated a new stage of social development aimed at the qualitative renewal of Soviet society and at restructuring.

On starting this essentially revolutionary work on an unprecedented scale, far from everyone involved in it was aware of the difficulties awaiting us on the chosen path. But one thing was clear: We could not live in the old way. The country had begun to lose momentum, unresolved problems were building up, elements of social corrosion had become apparent, and trends alien to socialism had emerged. All this had resulted in stagnation and pre-crisis phenomena.

The analytical work done by the party, the discussion of its results at the 27th CPSU Congress, the Congress decisions, progressive sociopolitical thinking—all these clearly indicated that fundamentally new approaches were needed in all spheres. In the economy and the social sphere, in the management of the economy and society, in the spiritual sphere and in encouraging the activity and initiative of the working people. This was the only way we could hold on to what had been gained through the labor and heroism of the preceding generations, it was the only way we could give a new boost to the development of our socialist society.

The conclusion of the party, the people, and of all who feel profoundly and sincerely for the country, for socialism, and for our common future was unanimous: There is no alternative to restructuring. We could reject or even defer restructuring only at very great cost both to our society's internal development and to the international positions of the Soviet state and socialism as a whole. This real truth was stated bluntly and frankly, with facts and figures at hand.

Three years have passed. They have seen a great deal. The concept, strategy and tactics of restructuring have been drawn up. Its revolutionary principles have been clearly defined: more democracy, more socialism. Restructuring today is social practice.

Restructuring as a way of thinking and acting is gaining an increasingly strong hold on the masses and becoming more and more deeply a part of life, determining the nature of social consciousness and of practical work.

We have changed over the past three years. We have raised our heads and straightened up, we look the facts honestly in the face, we speak aloud and openly of painful things, and together we are seeking ways to resolve problems which have built up over decades. The real changes which have already become apparent in the resolution of a number of social and economic tasks would be impossible without a decisive shift toward democratization.

We are all learning to live under conditions of broadening democracy and *glasnost'* and are undergoing a great learning process. It is no easy learning process. It has proved harder than we presumed to rid ourselves of old thoughts and actions. But the chief thing uniting us today is the awareness that there is no going back. The pernicious nature of such an action is obvious.

How are we to revive more quickly the Leninist essence of socialism, purge it of accretions and deformations, and rid ourselves of what was fettering society and preventing the full realization of socialism's potential? Precisely this is the problem on which, in the final analysis, the attention of the debate participants is focused, and diametrically opposed approaches are sometimes manifested here.

Now that we have embarked on the second stage of restructuring, questions to which answers already seemed to have been given have once again become topical. They include, above all, this one—can we not get by without breaking things, without radical measures, can we not confine ourselves just to improving what was created earlier? In the process of restructuring do we not risk losing or destroying much of what has been created over the seven decades since the Great October Socialist Revolution?

Many difficult, painful questions are being raised. *Glasnost'* has shown that the debate sometimes lacks political culture and the ability to listen to one another and to conduct a scientific analysis of social processes, or else there simply isn't enough knowledge and arguments.

And restructuring itself is frequently understood in different ways. One understanding is that it is just another cosmetic repair job. Others have seen restructuring as an opportunity for some kind of "dismantling" of the whole system of socialism, and if this is so, then the whole path traveled since the October Revolution is declared false, and the values and principles of socialism groundless. Yet others get carried away with radical phraseology, nurturing in themselves and others the illusion of skipping necessary stages.

Why do these questions arise, and what do they reflect? There are many reasons. Some people have not yet gotten to the bottom of what is happening. Some people are not fully aware of the seriousness of the situation which has taken shape. Some people doubt their own strength—and not only their own strength. Some people find it hard to part with spiritual laziness and tranquility and are unaccustomed to assuming the burden of taking responsibility for their actions. Some people have already managed to take fright at the scale of the transformations.

Such diversity of reactions to the practical business of restructuring is understandable, particularly if you take into account both the burden of former conservative habits and the complex and unaccustomed nature of the new problems concentrated in this brief, three-year stage. It is clear that it is necessary to further explain the ideas and aims of restructuring and the causes which gave rise to it, to investigate social processes collectively, and to separate the wheat from the chaff in both the old and the new. All this—we repeat—is normal and natural. The debate in society on all questions of our life is also natural. It is proceeding and will continue to develop. Its beneficial influence on social development is becoming increasingly noticeable.

The CPSU Central Committee February plenum concretized the party's new tasks in restructuring all spheres of life at the present stage. The plenum speech of General Secretary of the CPSU Central Committee M. S. Gorbachev, "Revolutionary Restructuring Requires Ideology of Renewal," made a clear analysis of today's problems and set forth a program of ideological support for restructuring. People want to be more aware of the meaning of the changes which have begun in society, to see the essence and significance of the proposed solutions, and to know what is meant by the new quality of society which we want to acquire. The struggle for restructuring is being waged both in production and in the spiritual sphere. And even though this struggle does not assume the form of class antagonisms, it is proceeding sharply. Attitudes are always exacerbated and judgments made when something new emerges.

The debate itself and its nature and thrust attest to the democratization of our society. The diversity of judgments, assessments and positions constitutes one of the most important signs of the times and attests to the socialist pluralism of opinions which really exists now.

But it is impossible not to notice a very specific dimension of this debate. It occasionally declares itself not by a desire to interpret and investigate what is happening nor by a wish to advance the cause but, on the contrary, to slow it down by shouting the usual incantations: "They are betraying ideals!"; "abandoning principles!"; "undermining foundations!"

I think that we are not just dealing here with sociopsychological phenomena. Such a stance has its roots in command- and edict-based bureaucratic management methods. It is also bound up with the moral legacy of the time as well as naked pragmatic interests and considerations and the desire to defend one's own privileges—whether material, social or spiritual—at any price.

It is an axiom of Marxism that ideas and interests are mutually linked categories. Any interest is expressed in certain ideas. Behind all ideas there is invariably a particular interest. Conservative opposition to restructuring is composed of the weight of custom and habitual thinking and action derived from the past along with the belligerent, selfish interests of those accustomed to living at others' expense and reluctant to kick the habit. It is against these interests that restructuring is objectively aimed, for restructuring, like every revolution, is not just for something, it is also against something. It is against everything that impedes our living a better, cleaner and fuller life, making more rapid progress and paying the least price for the inevitable mistakes and miscalculations that occur along the new path.

In this difficult situation it is necessary to clearly discern where there is real discussion, genuine concern over real problems and a search for the best answers and solutions, and where, on the other hand, there is a desire to turn democratization and *glasnost'* against themselves, against restructuring.

Some people have become mentally confused and perplexed. The launching of democratization, the rejection of edict- and command-based methods of leadership and management, the expansion of *glasnost'*, and the lifting of all manner of prohibitions and restrictions have generated apprehension: Are we not shaking the very foundations of socialism, revising the principles of Marxism-Leninism?

Some people maintain as follows: "We are heading for petty bourgeois socialism based on commodity-money relationships. And who is dragging it into our society? Idealists with a Menshevik mentality [*men'shinstvuyushchiye idealisty*: presumably this is author's rendition of more commonly encountered *men'shevistvuyushchiye idealisty* much criticized during the 1930s through the early 1950s]. That is the main danger for us and for world peace in general. That is the 20th-century plague which V. I. Lenin put so much effort into combatting.

"Don't rock the boat!" others say, intimidatingly. "You'll overturn and destroy socialism."

There are also those who bluntly propose stopping or else turning back altogether.

The long article "I Cannot Waive Principles" that appeared in the newspaper *Sovetskaya Rossiya* on March 13 was a reflection of such feelings.

The article, written in the form of a "Letter to the Editor," attracted readers' attention. It contains observations with which one is bound to agree. There is energetically expressed concern over certain negative phenomena. There is a heatedness of expression which also communicates itself to the reader.

But there is something else that is nevertheless more important: the reason it was written, the kind of solutions it proposes and the overall spirit and style of those solutions. It is by those criteria that the utter incompatibility and antithesis between the stances adopted in the article and the basic thrusts of restructuring are revealed.

Let us make a reservation here: Any author is entitled to defend his standpoint. And precisely this approach is now established in our society thanks to *glasnost'* and restructuring. It is the job of a press organ to present a particular stance for readers' judgment and to define its own attitude toward it. The rubric under which the article was published allowed one to suppose that a polemic on the nature of the questions raised would follow, if not immediately, then at least after a certain time. This is particularly necessary when the questions raised are serious and couched in a vein which can only be described as providing an ideological platform and manifesto for anti-restructuring forces. It is no wonder that many people are asking how the fact of this article's publication and the manner in which it was done are to be understood. Does it not signal, as has already occurred, a return to the old rut?

Whether the author intended it or not, the article is primarily aimed at artificially setting certain categories of Soviet people against one another, precisely at the moment when the unity of creative forces—despite all the shades of opinion—is more necessary than ever and when such unity is the prime requirement of restructuring and an absolute necessity simply for normal life, work and the constructive renewal of society. Herein resides the fundamental feature of restructuring, which is designed to unite the maximum number of like-minded people in the struggle against phenomena impeding our lives. Precisely and principally against the phenomena, not only and not simply against certain incorrigible proponents of bureaucracy, corruption, abuse and so forth. Not to strip everyone of their responsibilities, but to hunt out the "scapegoats."

Moreover, the article is not constructive. In an extensive, pretentiously-titled article essentially no space was found to work out a single problem of restructuring. Whatever was discussed—*glasnost'*, openness, the disappearance of areas free from criticism, youth—these processes and restructuring itself were linked only with difficulties and adverse consequences.

Perhaps readers saw for the first time in such a concentrated form in this "Letter to the Editor" not inquiry, not reflection, not even simply an expression of perplexity or confusion in the face of the complex and acute problems which life poses, but the nonacceptance of the very idea of renewal, a rigorous exposition of a highly defined stance, an essentially conservative and dogmatic stance.

In point of fact there are two basic theses running through the contents of the article: Why all this restructuring, and haven't we gone too far in questions of democratization and *glasnost'*? The article urges us to amend and adjust restructuring, otherwise, it is alleged, "people in authority" will have to rescue socialism.

It is evident that we are far from having everyone clearly realize the dramatic nature of the situation the country found itself in by April 1985, a situation which today we rightfully describe as pre-crisis. It is evident that everyone is not yet fully aware that administrative edict methods are totally obsolete. It is time that anyone who is still placing hopes in these methods or in their modification understood that all this has already been tried, tried repeatedly at that, and failed to produce the desired results. Any ideas about the simplicity and effectiveness of these methods are nothing but an illusion without any historical justification.

So, how is socialism to be "saved" today?

Should authoritarian methods and the practice of blind obedience and stifling of initiative be retained? Should we retain the system whereby bureaucratism, lack of control, corruption, bribery and petty bourgeois degeneration flourished lavishly?

Or should we revert to the Leninist principles whose essence is democratism, social justice, economic accountability and respect for the individual's honor, life and dignity? Do we have the right, in the face of the real difficulties and unsatisfied needs of the people, to adhere to the same old approaches which prevailed in the thirties and forties? Has not the time come to clearly differentiate between the essence of socialism and the historically restricted forms of its implementation? Has not the time come for a scientifically critical investigation of our history, primarily in order to change the world in which we are living and to learn harsh lessons for the future?

The item published by *Sovetskaya Rossiya* virtually advocates the first option. The second option is dictated by life, which also posed the demand for restructuring.

It is our ideological adversaries who are banking on identifying the essence of socialism with the old thinking, authoritarian methods and retreat from the principles of socialism. Surely it is obvious that in this context the positions taken by home-grown "mourners of socialism" coincide with the positions of socialism's opponents abroad? Surely, by scraping the rust of bureaucratism off the values, ideals and principles of socialism and cleansing it of all that is inhuman, we are releasing the best constructive forces for the struggle for socialism, for our values and our ideals? Surely the struggle against conservative thinking and dogmatism is a struggle for these ideals, against their distortion, and simultaneously against a lack of ideological discrimination and nihilism? After all, it is the blind, die-hard, undoubting dogmatists, whose nervous system is used to functioning strictly according to the principle of all or nothing, whereby everything is either harmonious and good or falling apart and bad, and who are likely to end up in a state of dismay and hysteria. It is they, incapable of withstanding the "tension of contradictions" and having lost their customary material and spiritual comforts, who turn into extreme nihilists before anybody else.

The article lacks the main element which defines a scientific approach toward matters: a desire to reveal the essence of historical processes and to separate the objective from the subjective, the necessary from the incidental, the things which really served the cause of socialism from those which harmed it, both in our own eyes and in the eyes of the whole world. The article is dominated by an essentially fatalistic perception of history which is totally removed from a genuinely scientific perception of it, by a tendency to justify everything that has happened in history in terms of historical necessity. The attitude that you can't make an omelette without breaking eggs is incompatible with both genuine science and socialist morality.

Almost half of the article is devoted to an assessment of our distant and recent history. The last few years provide graphic proof of the growing interest in the past shown by the broadest strata of the population. The principles of scientific historicism and truth are increasingly the basis on which the people's historical awareness is taking shape. At the same time, there are instances of people playing on the idea of patriotism. Those who loudly scream about alleged "internal threats" to socialism, those who join certain political extremists and look everywhere for internal enemies, "counterrevolutionary nations" and so on, are not patriots. The patriots are those who act in the country's interests and for the people's benefit, without fearing any difficulties. We do not need contemplative or verbal patriotism, we need creative patriotism. Not nostalgic and backward-looking [*kvasnoy i lapotnyy*] patriotism, but the patriotism of socialist transformations. Patriotism based not only on love for the area of your birth but imbued with pride in the accomplishments of the great motherland of socialism.

The past is vitally necessary for the present, for solving the tasks of restructuring. Life's objective demand—"More socialism!"—makes it incumbent upon us to investigate what we did yesterday and how we did it. What has to be rejected, what has to be retained. Which principles and values ought to be considered really socialist? And if today we are taking a critical look at our history, we are doing so only because we want a better and more complete idea of our path into the future.

We are reinstating the truth, cleansing it of the false and sly truths which led to the blind alley of public apathy; we are learning the lesson in truth taught by the 27th CPSU Congress. But the truth has proved bitter in many respects. An attempt is already being made to whitewash the past, to justify political deformities and crimes against socialism with references to nothing but emergency conditions.

Today we know: Many thousands of Communists and non-party people, economic and military cadres, scientists and cultural figures were subjected to mass repressions. . . . This is the truth, it is unavoidable. The party has spoken bluntly about this. Many accusations have already been dropped, and thousands and thousands of innocent people who suffered have been fully rehabilitated. The restoration of justice is continuing. As is well known, a Central Committee Politburo commission is at work, studying all aspects of facts and documents referring to these issues.

To keep silent about painful issues in our history means to

disregard the truth and show disrespect for the memory of those innocent victims of illegality and arbitrariness. There is just one truth. What is needed is complete clarity, accuracy and consistency as a moral guideline for the future.

Numerous discussions taking place today sharply raise the question of I. V. Stalin's role in our country's history. The article in *Sovetskaya Rossiya* does not overlook him, either. While declaring support for the CPSU Central Committee resolution on overcoming the personality cult and its consequences (1956) and approval for the assessment of Stalin's activity contained in the party's latest documents, in practice the article makes an attempt to refute them and to separate socialism and morality.

To suit his purpose the author turns to Churchill for support. Let us note: The eulogy of Stalin he quotes did not originate with Churchill. Something along these lines was said by the famous British Trotskyite I. Deutscher. Be that as it may, though, it would be legitimate to ask: Is it tactful to turn indiscriminately to bourgeois sources when assessing leaders and eminent figures of our party and state? Especially if we already have a clearly stated position by the party itself or, in this specific case, an assessment by V. I. Lenin.

Stalin's personality was extremely contradictory. Hence the furious arguments. But principled assessments were made at the 20th and 22nd Party Congresses and in the report "October and Restructuring: The Revolution Continues" by M. S. Gorbachev, general secretary of the CPSU Central Committee. Maintaining our positions of historic truth, we must see both Stalin's indisputable contribution to the struggle for socialism and the defense of socialist gains on the one hand, and, on the other hand, his flagrant political errors and the arbitrary rule permitted by him and his entourage, for which our people paid a great price and which had serious consequences for our society's life. People can sometimes be heard to claim that Stalin did not know about acts of lawlessness. He did not just know about them, he organized and directed them. That is now a proven fact. And Stalin's guilt—along with that of his closest entourage—before the party and people for the mass repressions and lawlessness he permitted is enormous and unforgivable.

Yes, all historians are molded by specific socioeconomic, ideological and political conditions. But the cult was not inevitable. It is alien to the nature of socialism and only became possible because of deviations from fundamental socialist principles.

But why—now that the party has provided a clear and direct answer to this question—should we return to it again and again? I think for two reasons. Primarily because, in defending Stalin, people thereby defend the retention in our life and practice today of the methods engendered by him for "resolving" disputed questions and of the social and state structures and norms of party and social life he created. The main point is that they are defending the right to arbitrary rule. Arbitrary rule, which, on closer inspection, invariably turns out to be just an egoistic interest—although in some people this interest can be aimed at taking more and giving less, while in others it is wrapped up in the outwardly respectable garb of claims to a monopoly in science or to one's own infallibility, or to something else.

Another reason to keep coming back to the question of Stalin's personality is that there is speculation around this assessment of what people hold most dear—the meaning of the lives they have led. Concepts get substituted: If Stalin was guilty of crimes, people claim, how are we to assess our past achievements? How are we to assess the labor and heroism of people who caused the land of socialism to achieve historic gains? Are we not denying them too in condemning Stalin and rejecting his methods?

No we are not, we are actually extolling them even further. An honest worker, a soldier in the battlefield, any Soviet individual who through his work proved his patriotism and his devotion to the motherland and socialism through their work was doing—and did!—his duty. It was his work, selflessness and heroism that brought our country to unprecedented heights. And only an immoral person would cast aspersions on the people's work and achievements. But today we are more aware than ever of how difficult it was to do real work at that time—a time that was difficult in every respect.

It would be wrong now to put these people down as advocates of Stalin's lawlessness. It would also be wrong because we realize and are obliged to realize just how much greater the results of their efforts would have been for the whole country and for each of us if their creative input and material effectiveness had not been impaired by objectively anti-Leninist and antisocialist practices.

No, the lives of party, war and labor veterans were not in vain! All subsequent generations owe them a debt that can never be repaid.

But some people just cannot rid themselves of nostalgia for the past, when certain people would speak and others would listen and submissively do their bidding. Certain people's nostalgia can be understood, but it is not a press organ's job to propagandize such sentiments, not only by not making a proper assessment of them, but by creating the impression among people that they are being offered some kind of "new" political platform.

One's attention is also drawn to the author's arguments on the class approach to the assessment of the arguments and opinions expressed in the discussions. The author's view is that certain controversial positions that people may adopt are not engendered by problems but by people's definite social or national provenance. This thereby focuses the question not on what is being said and disputed, but on who precisely is doing the saying and disputing.

A class approach is undoubtedly needed in discussions. But even in those cases where we are forced to deal with people who have ideas alien to socialism, the class approach is not a "hallmark" that makes "selection" easier, but a tool of scientific analysis. The article states that the "descendants of the classes overthrown by October are alive and well" along with the "spiritual heirs of Dan and Martov and other Russian Social Democrats, the spiritual followers of Trotsky or Yagoda, and the descendants of NEPmen, basmaches and kulaks." The article is virtually prepared to seek a genetic reason for antisocialist sentiments. Is this position consonant with Stalin's well-known directive on the exacerbation of the class struggle in the process of socialist building—a directive which had tragic consequences?

The article expresses concern about the well-known spread of nihilism among a section of our young people. Should this be a cause for concern? Yes. But it should be seen that today's "distortions" in young people's consciousness are symptoms of what is by no means a modern disease. This disease is rooted in the past. It is the consequence of the spiritual diet that we fed to young people for decades and of the discrepancies between what was said on rostrums and what actually happened in real life.

The best teacher of restructuring—the one to whom we should constantly listen—is life, and life is dialectical. We should constantly remember the words of Engels that there is nothing that has been unconditionally established once and for all as sacrosanct. It is this continual motion and the constant renewal of nature, society and our thinking that is the point of departure and the initial, most cardinal principle in our thinking.

At the most complex, dramatic and crucial moments in history V. I. Lenin again and again turned to dialectics as the living soul of Marxism; he did so not only to understand the historic events himself, but also to arm the party and the popular masses with this concept. This was the same idea that produced the concept of restructuring.

Restructuring is gaining pace. That is obvious. The very atmosphere of society and the way people feel are different. On the whole, workers, kolkhoz members, and the intelligentsia act with a sense of responsibility for the cause of restructuring, for the country and for socialism. And we should not be scared about movements of ideas or quests for the best ways of realizing the potential of socialist democracy. This is particularly necessary now, in the period of preparations for the 19th All-Union Party Conference.

Let us return to the question: What has been done already? How are the party's course and the decisions of the 27th CPSU Congress and Central Committee plenums being implemented? What positive changes are taking place in people's lives?

We have really gotten down to tackling the most pressing, priority problems—housing, food, the supply of goods and services to the population. A turn toward accelerated development of the social sphere has begun. Concrete decisions have been adopted on restructuring education and health care. The radical economic reform—our main lever for implementing large-scale transformations—is being put into practice. "That is the main political result of the last three years," M. S. Gorbachev said at the Fourth All-Union Congress of Kolkhoz Members.

The voice of the intelligentsia and all the working people has begun to make itself heard powerfully and strongly in society's spiritual life. This is one of the first gains accomplished by restructuring. Democratism is impossible without freedom of thought and speech, without the open, broad clash of opinions, without keeping a critical eye on our life.

Our intelligentsia has done much to prepare public awareness to understand the need for profound, cardinal changes. It has itself become actively involved in restructuring. It takes up the best traditions created by its predecessors, calls for conscience, morality and decency,and upholds humanist principles and socialist norms of life.

How many words have been spoken and written about unifying the intelligentsia with the working class and kolkhoz peasantry. And with what new light these truths now shine, at a time of nationwide support for restructuring from the broad masses of working people, in a period in which genuinely patriotic, moral assessments of thoughts, deeds and the whole of our life are united in all strata of society. How many patriotic initiatives in restructuring are associated with the names of our writers and poets, dramatists and critics. Here we should recall the brilliant, aggressive journalistic writing, imbued with the ideology of renewal, of I. Vasilyev, which has found such a worthy place in the pages of that same *Sovetskaya Rossiya,* among the ranks of the best materials on restructuring.

But we see something else too: In certain works there is a lack of shared experience with the people, their history, their joys and griefs. Some authors, as if they were apostles of truth, pontificate and instruct everyone on what must be done and how. There are many attempts to make one's mark cause a sensation, and amuse oneself with "facts" and "snippets," not for the sake of truth, but to suit one's own insatiable pride. This leads to juggling with facts, misrepresenting them, and—most important—it substitutes the history of the leadership's errors for the history of the people. Naturally, this approach offends the sensibilities of millions of honest people and does not help us to draw objective, useful lessons from history.

The roots of such phenomena lie in that same legacy of stagnation. People's thoughts and feelings were seething even then, as they reflected on what was happening and its consequences for the future. But people were forced to keep to themselves the results of this analysis, the outcome of their quest and their own proposals. Now all this bursts out into the open with an energy multiplied by years without *glasnost'*, and this does not always happen in a thoughtful and responsible way.

Culture is also subject to renewal and cleansing. The more profoundly and actively the intelligentsia is involved in the life of the people and party, the quicker this process will become. Tact, good will, respect, recognition of the right to one's own opinion, but also the honest, competent, open identification of errors—that is what many party committees lack today in their work with the intelligentsia. "On questions of culture," V. I. Lenin stressed, "haste and recklessness are more harmful than anything" (Vol. 45, p. 389).

A different phenomenon is sometimes observed in the practice of party work. This can be seen particularly clearly in examples of attitudes toward the critical voice of the press. Some people are prepared to see all the troubles, all the unpleasantness of daily life in the fact that the newspapers "have gotten out of hand, express opinions about everything, stir up public opinion," and so forth. It must be recognized that a newspaper column is a secondary phenomenon. The primary phenomenon is in life itself! If we are not to read about shortcomings in newspaper columns, they must not exist in life.

Once again we see the value, the responsibility, of the printed word. How sometimes unverified facts or claims to a monopoly of the truth, and sometimes simply the attempt to adapt the facts to fit a concept formulated beforehand by the author, tend to backfire against the very best intentions. Conservatives represent such errors as absolutes, they reduce the fruits of democratism and *glasnost'* to them alone. And what is the result? Forces which at first glance are diametrically opposed in their convictions are united into one bloc, in practice, in retarding restructuring.

There are no prohibited topics today. Journals, publishing houses and studios decide for themselves what to publish. But the appearance of the article "I Cannot Waive Principles" is an attempt to revise party decisions little by little. It has been said repeatedly at meetings in the party Central Committee that the Soviet press is not a private concern, that Communists writing for the press and editors should have a sense of responsibility for articles and publications. In this case the newspaper *Sovetskaya Rossiya*, which, let us be frank, has done much for restructuring, departed from this principle.

Debates, discussions and polemics are, of course, necessary. They lie in store for us in the future too. There are also many pitfalls in store for us, traps laid by the past. We must all work together to clear these traps from our path. We need disputes which help to advance restructuring and lead to the consolidation of forces, to cohesion around restructuring, and not to disunity.

It is less than three months until the 19th All-Union Party Conference. That is a great event in the life of the party and all the people. Preparations are under way. The main thing is to bring to the conference the experience of restructuring and an analysis of how the concept of restructuring is being implemented in practice and what results it is yielding. In order to really see what is happening, the new phenomena in life, Communists must be in control of events and not tag along in their wake. V. I. Lenin said repeatedly: "A firm line by the party, its unswerving determination is also a factor in determining the mood, especially at the most critical revolutionary moments . . ." (Vol. 34, pp. 411–412). Restructuring is the cause of every Communist, the patriotic duty of every citizen.

More light. More initiative. More responsibility. A more rapid mastery of the full profundity of the Marxist-Leninist concept of restructuring, of the new political thinking. We can and must revive the Leninist practice of the socialist society—the most humane, the most just. We will firmly and steadily follow the revolutionary principles of restructuring: more *glasnost'*, more democracy, more socialism.

About the Authors

John Edwin Mroz, President and the co-founder of the Institute for East-West Security Studies, is a foreign policy specialist dealing with Soviet, East European and Third World affairs. A graduate of the Fletcher School of Law and Diplomacy, he has served as a consultant to the Department of State, industry and foundations on international political and security matters. The author of *Beyond Security* and numerous published articles in Europe and North America, he previously served as Executive Vice President of the International Peace Academy, where he was responsible for establishing peace-keeping training programs in Latin America, Africa and the Middle East.

Academician Abel Aganbegyan is currently Head of the Economics Branch of the USSR Academy of Sciences and General Secretary Mikhail S. Gorbachev's chief economic advisor. He has been a corresponding member of the USSR Academy of Sciences since 1964. After graduating from the Moscow State Institute of Economics in 1955, he worked until 1961 for the State Committee of the Council of Ministers of the USSR. He was named the Director of the Institute of Economics and Organization of Industrial Production of the Siberian Section of the Academy of Sciences of the USSR in 1966, after having served as their laboratory chief since 1961. His most recent publications include *The Economic Challenge of Perestroika* (Bloomington: Indiana University Press, 1988).

Professor Timor Timofeyev has been Director of the Institute of International Labor Studies at the USSR Academy of Sciences since 1966. From 1961 to 1966, he was Deputy Director of the Institute for World Economy and International Relations. Professor Timofeyev, a historian and economist, has published numerous studies on Soviet domestic and foreign affairs.

For Product Safety Concerns and Information please contact our EU representative GPSR@taylorandfrancis.com Taylor & Francis Verlag GmbH, Kaufingerstraße 24, 80331 München, Germany

Batch number: 10732742

Printed by Printforce, the Netherlands